WILDLIFE RESCUE

Alternative To Extinction

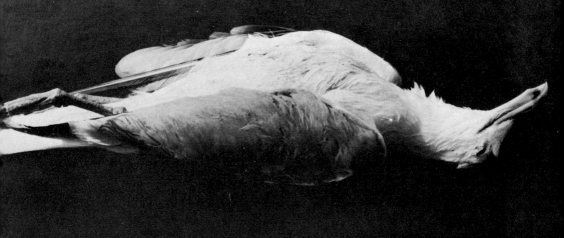

WILDLIFE RESCUE

Alternative To Extinction

By Ada and Frank Graham, Jr.

COWLES BOOK COMPANY, INC.
NEW YORK

Copyright © 1970 by Ada and Frank Graham, Jr.
SBN 402-14081-8
Library of Congress Catalog Card Number 72-104362
Cowles Book Company, Inc.
A subsidiary of Cowles Communications, Inc.
Published simultaneously in Canada by
  General Publishing Company, Ltd.
  30 Lesmill Road, Don Mills, Toronto, Ontario
Printed in the United States of America
First Edition

CONTENTS

Introduction

Modern man thinks he needs more machines, more roads, more parking lots, more airports, and more big buildings. This is what many people call progress. But in clearing the land or in killing wild creatures to feed and clothe ourselves, we often forget that we are taking out of the world much of what makes it worth living in. We leave no room for the other creatures who share our life on this planet. It is important to find people who care about saving them.

That is why the four people in our book are special. At first they may not seem at all alike. Their personalities, their ages, and their styles of living have little in common. But in one sense they are all very much alike. Each one expresses, by his or her way of life, a deep concern for living things—both at his doorstep and at the opposite end of the world.

We carried a tape recorder with us when we visited three of these people and recorded their stories. We learned that they had loved wild creatures from the time they were children and carried this love with them when they grew up. Then they found ways in which they could help to rescue them in a world that did not always seem to care about wildlife anymore. The place did not matter. Each person rescued animals in the place where he or she could do it best—in the jungles of South America, on the beautiful Pacific coast, or in the heart of New York City.

We could not record the voice of the fourth person, Guy Bradley, because he lived many years ago. So we visited the Everglades, which was his home and which he helped to protect with his life. And we read a diary written by a friend of his, which tells the story of a trip that Guy Bradley made when he was a boy. At first, wild birds were things for him to kill. As he came to know them, his feelings about them changed. And that is why we still remember him.

The will to work for what they cared about is what makes these people's lives special. This is what makes their stories and what they know about plants and animals so important today when wild things are in trouble all over the world. And that is what made us want to put their stories into a book.

Ada and Frank Graham, Jr.
Milbridge, Maine

Plume Birds

Late in the winter of 1885 Guy and Louis Bradley of Lake Worth, Florida, were asked the sort of question that calls a boy to adventure.

"I'm going off plume hunting for a month in my sloop," Charles Pierce, a friend of theirs, told them. "Do you want to come with me?"

It was not a difficult question for the Bradley brothers to answer. Of course they would go. Guy was only sixteen years old at the time, and Louis was not much older, but they had spent a good deal of their young lives hunting and fishing in the woods and rivers around Lake Worth. Both were fine marksmen. And both wanted to see more of the untamed country and its wildlife.

Charles Pierce, who was twenty years old, made a perfect companion for the Bradleys. He loved the outdoors, too. His uncle had recently asked him to become the captain and caretaker of a sturdy sailing vessel called the *Bonton*. Pierce had dreamed for a long time about a trip down the coast and into the interior of southern Florida.

"Boys," he said once, "the game is getting just awful scarce nowadays. The trouble is the country is getting all settled up. Too much civilization for good hunting anymore."

The best hunting was in remote sections of southern Florida, where no one ever went but plume hunters and Indians. The plume hunters shot herons, egrets, and other wading birds, and sold their beautiful feathers for use as ornaments on women's hats.

The long feathers of the egret were highly prized by plume hunters.

What kind of sport was it, we might ask today, to shoot these big, slow-moving birds? For the boys, the answer was that plume hunting was "man's work." They would be going into some of the wildest country on the North American continent to shoot birds whose feathers were worth a great deal of money. There was no law in 1885 against hunting the birds. The trip they were setting out on was entirely legal.

On the morning of March 11, Guy and Louis Bradley went aboard the boat that was to take them on their adventure. The *Bonton* was a sloop—that is, it had a single mast on which the mainsail was hoisted, and a smaller sail forward of the mast called a jib. There would be plenty of room for the three boys. The sloop was twenty-eight feet long with a beam, or width, of seven feet, and it had a roomy cabin.

Charles Pierce had built a small canvas canoe to use when they wanted to explore small streams. He lashed it to the deck of the *Bonton*. The Bradleys also had built a canoe for the trip. The called it the *Ibis*, after one of the plume birds they would hunt. Because it was too large to bring aboard, they decided to tow it behind the *Bonton*.

We know a great deal about this trip because Charles Pierce kept a diary. Every evening he wrote down an account of that day's events. He tells us that, before leaving on their adventure, he and the Bradleys sailed over to Palm Beach to collect supplies.

"Stopped at Dr. Potter's place to get some medicine," Pierce wrote, "got laudanum and

quinine, then went on to the Brelsford's store and bought some kerosene, vinegar, cocoa, onions, and fish hooks. We stopped at the post office to get a bottle to put my vinegar in."

Then they hoisted the sails and the *Bonton* glided out into the Atlantic Ocean. They were on their own, bound for a strange wilderness that few men even twice their age had seen. As the *Bonton* passed Lake Worth on her way down the coast, a man who knew the boys saluted them by raising the flag on his flagpole. They proudly replied by running a flag up the *Bonton*'s masthead.

But it was not smooth sailing. The seas were rough and the winds against them. Soon the winds died altogether and the *Bonton* lost her forward motion.

"We had to anchor to keep the Gulf Stream from taking us back up the coast," Charles Pierce wrote in his diary.

It took them two days to reach the inlet at the mouth of the Hillsboro River where they planned to begin hunting. The sky was so dark when they arrived that Pierce paddled ahead of the *Bonton* in the tiny *Ibis,* searching for the inlet to the river. The Bradleys lowered the *Bonton*'s sails. Guided by Pierce, they poled the big sloop into a safe harbor at the river's mouth.

"On getting up this morning," Pierce wrote in his diary, "we found the schooner *Neff* at anchor near us. Her captain is an old friend of mine and we went to call on him. He had killed a deer the day before and gave us a ham from the deer, which was fine eating."

Corkscrew Swamp is similar to the wilderness visited by Guy Bradley.

The Hillsboro was a shallow river. The boys found this out when they ran aground. So they decided to look for a good hiding place for the *Bonton* and go exploring by canoe. They discovered a winding side channel where the mangrove trees were tall and thick and no one would be able to see the sloop from the river. Pierce and the Bradleys loaded their canoes with supplies, tents, and guns, and set off toward Cypress Creek.

Soon they entered the strangest country they had ever seen. The creek flowed through a broad open swamp. The water was so shallow that they had to get out of the canoes and push them through the thick clumps of saw grass and lily pads.

"While we were at this work I stepped on an alligator," Pierce wrote. "The gator gave a furious wriggle and I nearly fell on my back trying to get away from him. He came to the top and tried to bite my canoe. I then grabbed up my gun and killed him."

The work became harder now. The boys learned that the only way to get through the saw grass in the channel was to stand on it until it sank beneath their weight. Then they were able to push their canoes over the top of the grass. At every turn they saw alligators, which showed no fear of them and took their time moving out of the way.

There was no dry land in sight, so Pierce and the Bradleys prepared to spend the night sleeping in their canoes. They were beginning to grow discouraged. They had come so far and worked so hard, yet the plume birds still eluded them.

It was just at dusk that they caught sight of the birds for the first time. They could see large flocks—herons, egrets, and ibises—flying overhead, bound for their rookery, or gathering place, farther along the creek.

Now they knew the nesting birds were close by. In the morning the boys paddled on, passing through a forest of cypress trees whose trunks stood in the still water. Tangles of Spanish moss hung in curtains from the upper branches, blotting out the sun.

The young hunters came upon the rookery as they rounded a bend in the creek. The birds were perched in the trees, many of them on their nests. In his diary, Charles Pierce described the slaughter in the rookery.

"We immediately went into it and commenced to shoot the birds," he wrote. "About three o'clock we had cleaned it up. Louis killed seven white herons. Guy killed two herons and a wood ibis. I killed six white herons and one egret."

When they had killed some of the birds and driven the others away, the boys continued along the creek. They came upon another rookery and opened fire again. Louis killed four birds, Guy killed three, and Pierce killed eight. Then it became too dark to shoot and the boys camped for the night.

They stayed in the area for several days. At times they had to get out of their canoes because the creek had become impassable. They simply plunged into water and mud up to their knees and pushed the canoes through thick masses of plants called water lettuce.

Their food was almost gone. They ate

mostly the fish they caught and the small animals and birds they shot. Once Guy Bradley went off by himself. The others heard a shot. When they finally caught up with him, they found him sitting on the ground with a big smile on his face and a dead wild turkey on the ground beside him. He had shot the first turkey he had ever seen!

Charles Pierce came upon the remains of an old canoe that had been partly burned. It was made in the Indian manner—light, narrow, and built so that it could be poled through the shallow, plant-filled waters with ease. Pierce discovered that he could navi-

A young alligator swims through a Florida swamp.

gate the old canoe by standing in the un-
burned end, and he set out alone to explore
the swamp.

"I ran into a bunch of alligators," he tells
us. "There must have been 50 of them, perhaps more. Because gators eat wounded
plume birds we've always made a practice
of killing them whenever we get a chance.
And here was a chance too good to let pass.
Although my shot was too small for good
work on gators I opened fire on them. I don't
know how many I killed because as soon as
my 15 shells were used up I got out of there
as soon as possible."

In the evenings the boys prepared their
bird skins, cooked their supper, and talked
about the wonderful things they had seen
during the day. One evening just before dark
two scarlet ibises flew over their camp.
"They were out of reach of our guns," Pierce
wrote, "so all we could do was to admire
their beauty and watch them go."

The nights themselves were never quiet.
Once, while the boys slept, a possum got into
the box in which they kept their prize
plumes. The animal destroyed two of them.
Another time a noise close by awakened
them as they slept in their canoes. They
raised their heads to see what it was.

There, in the moonlight, they saw a giant
bull alligator feasting on the bodies of the
plume birds they had skinned earlier in the
evening. Guy reached for his gun. But the
alligator heard his movement. With a twitch
of its great tail it whirled and disappeared
into the swamp.

The boys had been away from the *Bonton* for almost three weeks. Now they decided to turn back. Once more they struggled through the swamp.

"We went down to the nesting place that we shot out on our way up," Pierce wrote in his diary. "We found the birds nearly all gone. I managed to kill one. Guy killed an alligator. Then we stopped to fish for brim [bream, a variety of sunfish]. Louis and Guy caught 45 and I caught 17. They were very small, otherwise we would have had more fish than we could eat."

They found the *Bonton* just where they had left it. For a while they sailed along the coast and then entered a creek that wound through the Everglades. This time the water was deep enough for them to remain in the sloop. They made their way through the vast sea of saw grass, following a "burn" started by the Indians to mark the channel. For another week they sailed from one rookery to the next and killed every bird they could.

Allan D. Cruikshank–National Audubon Society

After being "shot out" in the early 1900 s, Cuthbert Rookery has again become a nesting place for plume birds.

At the end of that week it was time for the three friends to separate. Charles Pierce had agreed to rent the *Bonton* to a professional plume hunter. Guy and Louis Bradley planned to return to Lake Worth.

"Louis and Guy took their belongings from the *Bonton* this morning and stored them in the *Ibis*," Pierce wrote in his diary. "I felt lonesome after the boys left, and went to work so that I would not think about being alone."

The Bradleys' adventure was over.

Nearly twenty years passed. Great changes came over Florida in that time. The great flights of plume birds over the swamps and forests were seldom seen anymore.

The spectacular quality of the birds had caused their undoing. For many centuries, human beings have admired the beauty of birds. Indians, princes, and fashionable women have traditionally used feathers as ornaments. But this desire to decorate oneself with plumes—the long, showy feathers of birds—reached its peak in the nineteenth century. Hardly a woman's hat was made that did not carry feathers on it—and sometimes the whole wings and heads of birds!

As plume birds became scarce, the hunters began to kill even the small songbirds of parks and gardens for their feathers. An *ornithologist*—a scientist who studies birds—walked through the shopping district of New York City one afternoon in the 1890s. He was curious to see what women were wearing on their hats. He counted 700 hats, and 542 of them were decorated with feathers. Among them he recognized the feathers of forty different species of birds. Some were the large plumes of wading birds, while others were the small feathers of bluebirds, warblers, woodpeckers, and owls.

A magazine writer in 1886 had this to say about the fashion:

"We read in a newspaper the other day that Mrs. Jones had her gown of unrelieved black looped up with blackbirds; and a winged creature so dusky that it could have been nothing else but a crow reposed among the curls and braids of her hair. Perhaps if the lady in question could have seen the crow during its lifetime perched upon and feeding on the decaying carcass of a horse, she might have objected to the association."

The birds that grow the most spectacular feathers in North America live mostly in the southern states. They are wading birds with long legs and long plumes. These birds—herons, egrets, and ibises—were called plume birds by the men who hunted them. They provided many of the *aigrettes,* or sprays of plumes, that decorated women's hats and dresses.

These graceful plumes were eagerly sought by *milliners*—people who manufacture hats for women. They paid large numbers of hunters to go into the Everglades to kill plume birds, just as Charles Pierce and the Bradley brothers had killed them in 1885. By 1900 the price for the finest plumes had risen to thirty-two dollars an ounce. This was twice the price of gold at the time.

A 1914 magazine shows hats decorated with plume bird feathers.

The prices that milliners paid for plume birds varied a great deal, though. A milliner would pay only ten cents for the plumes of the Louisiana heron. Charles Pierce tells us in his diary that this bird's plumes weren't very pretty. "The bird was mostly good for eating," Pierce says. But the plumes from a great white heron were worth twenty-five dollars apiece. This large, stately bird was not plentiful to begin with, and the plume hunters almost wiped it out in Florida.

Hunters killed the plume birds mostly in the spring while they were tending their nests. At this time of year the birds grow their *nuptial plumes*—the long, brightly colored feathers that help to attract female birds. These plumes brought the most money on the market.

It was easy to hunt plume birds during the nesting season because they gathered in large numbers at the rookeries. When the hunters opened fire, the birds often did not fly away, but remained in the area where their young lay huddled in the nests. Hunters were able to kill the adult birds by the hundreds.

Later, after the hunters had taken the plumes and left the carcasses to rot in the blazing Florida sun, no adult birds remained alive to feed their young. Helpless, the young birds starved in their nests. None grew to lay eggs in future years and restore the once great flocks to their former numbers.

Hunters killed millions of birds in the United States every year for "fashion." Many people became alarmed by the rapid decline of the plume birds. They feared that those

Newly hatched egrets wait to be fed.

birds would disappear forever, as the passenger pigeon and several other kinds of birds had during the nineteenth century.

A strong feeling that the traffic in these beautiful birds was wrong began to spread across the county. Men, women, and children joined such clubs as the Audubon Societies to fight for strong laws to save the birds. During the 1890s "Bird Day" became a part of the year's program in many schools.

After 1900 several clubs fighting for bird protection united to form the National Association of Audubon Societies. Florida had passed a law several years earlier that prohibited the shooting of plume birds. But no one enforced the law—there were no policemen in the swamps!

The Audubon Societies began a search for a warden to protect the few plume birds left in southern Florida. They asked their friends in that state to suggest a man who was fearless and who knew the country well. One man came strongly recommended—Guy Bradley.

Much had changed in Guy Bradley's life since he had joined his brother, Louis, and Charles Pierce on their adventurous cruise. His father had been appointed postmaster in the little fishing village of Flamingo at the southern tip of Florida. There Guy had married and become the father of two small children.

He was in his thirties now—a strong, deeply tanned outdoorsman with thinning, curly hair and a moustache. Like many other hunters, he had learned that he did not have to kill wild things to enjoy them. He took great pleasure in guiding photographers and nature students to remote rookeries in the Everglades where plume birds might still be seen. People called him the finest guide in that part of the country. His services were in great demand.

In 1902 the Audubon Societies hired Bradley as a warden to protect the rookeries. Many visitors to the Everglades later wrote books and articles in which they praised Bradley's skills as a guide and warden. Among them was Herbert K. Job, a famous photographer.

"We struck inland with our guide, Bradley, the game warden of Monroe County," Job wrote afterward, "to visit a lake that lay several miles through the mangrove swamp. There was no boat in the lonely lake, but

Bradley proposed to carry a canvas canoe. This we found hidden in the confines of the swamp.

"It weighed over 50 pounds, and as we pushed on hour after hour through the maze of mangrove roots and tropical jungle, following a trail so blind that we often lost it, I was amazed at the strength of the hardy pioneer who carried it—a man of only moderate weight and size. We took only an occasional rest, during one of which Bradley climbed to the nest of a Red-Shouldered Hawk in a slender tree. He brought the one young hawk down to me to photograph and returned it again to its home."

Job tells how Bradley led the way overland on their various trips through the "forbidding and awful wilderness." Often the guide had to slash a path with his hatchet through the tangled mangroves. At other times he touched a match to the dry, razor-sharp saw grass so they could pass through the Everglades' prairie. And always both Bradley and Job had to fight off the swarms of mosquitoes that made the trip a "torture."

"The insects were so numerous," Job writes, "I could not avoid mashing them between the films in packing my photographic plates."

But Job was finally rewarded for the hardships of the trip. Bradley led him to the last of the great gathering places of the plume birds in southern Florida—Cuthbert Rookery. The rookery was named for a plume hunter who had discovered it several years earlier. He had "shot out" the rookery at that time.

Guy Bradley.

But the rookery lay on a mangrove-covered island in the middle of a lake that was difficult to reach. Few men knew of its existence. After a while the birds returned to it.

Job was thrilled by the flights of herons, egrets, and ibises. It was one of the most spectacular wildlife gatherings remaining in North America. There, in the midst of this wild scene, Job saw the sign that Bradley had posted months before. The sign warned plume hunters that it was against the law to kill the birds. With Bradley's help, Job photographed the birds and their nests.

"Without the guide I am sure I could never have found my way out of that swamp, even after being led into it," Job wrote. "The trails wander off into the jungle and from lake to lake. They were as blind as though no human being had ever followed them. None but thorough-going enthusiasts should venture upon such a trip as that to Cuthbert Rookery. It was the most arduous thing I have ever attempted."

Other men told similar stories of their adventures in the swamps and forests with

Bradley. Even when guiding visitors to the Everglades, Bradley remained on the watch for plume hunters. But the plume hunters watched him, too. The country was vast— much too large for one man to protect. Sometimes the hunters waited for Bradley to leave a rookery. Then they would go in and kill the birds.

In 1904, Frank M. Chapman, an ornithologist, asked Bradley to take him to Cuthbert Rookery. But when they met Bradley had bad news for Chapman. Just after a recent visit by Bradley to the rookery, the plume hunters had gone in and "shot it out." All the birds had been killed or driven away.

"You could've walked right around the rookery on those birds' bodies—between four and five hundred of them," Bradley said.

Then he mentioned something that he had told Chapman several times before—Bradley expected the plume hunters to try to kill him.

The warden had good reason to believe this. Some of the hunters hated him. One of them, Walter Smith, was an especially dangerous man. Bradley had arrested Smith's son several times for killing birds. Smith had told the people of Flamingo that if Bradley ever again arrested any member of his family he would kill him.

But Bradley remained unafraid. He had seen the great flights of plume birds decline to a few small flocks. If they were not protected they would disappear from Florida very soon. He continued to do the job that the Audubon Societies paid him for—protecting those birds to the best of his ability.

"Bradley took a personal interest in his work," the president of the Audubon Societies once wrote, "and he was genuinely proud when he could report an increase in the birds' numbers."

On July 8, 1905, Bradley stepped out on the front porch of the little house where he lived in Flamingo. From there he could look across the intensely blue waters of Florida Bay to where a pair of porpoises were hunting fish in water so shallow it scarcely covered them. They were rounding up a school of mullet, just as cowboys herd steers on the range. The porpoises caught the fish in midair as they leaped from the water in an attempt to escape.

But Bradley's sharp eyes saw something besides the porpoises. Off on the horizon he made out the masts of a sailing ship. The ship, he guessed, belonged to Walter Smith. It was headed for a small island called Oyster Key, where a few plume birds gathered.

Bradley pushed his small boat into the water and rowed two miles to the key. He saw Smith's schooner—a kind of sailing ship—anchored nearby. He also heard shots on the key. As Bradley came near, Smith appeared on deck and fired a rifle into the air. Bradley knew that this was a signal for Smith's son to return to the schooner.

Bradley reached the schooner just as the younger Smith and a friend were climbing aboard. Each of them carried two dead egrets.

"What do you want, Bradley?" Smith called from the deck.

"I want to arrest your son," Bradley said.

"You need a warrant to arrest him."

"No," Bradley said. "I heard the shots and I saw him with the dead birds. I don't need a warrant if I catch him in the act."

"Well, if you want him you have to come aboard and get him."

"Put down that rifle, Smith, and I'll come aboard," Bradley said.

The warden moved his small boat closer to the schooner. Smith raised his rifle and fired. The bullet hit Bradley in the chest, killing him instantly. His body drifted for twenty-four hours in the small boat before it was found by the people of Flamingo.

Bradley's murderer was never convicted. A trial was held. Witnesses aboard Smith's schooner told of the events that led to the shooting. But no one would admit seeing the fatal shot fired. The jury, many of whom were Smith's friends, preferred to believe the murderer's story that he had killed Bradley only after the warden had shot at him. Though experts proved that Bradley's gun had not been fired, Smith was set free.

But the murder at Oyster Key made a deep impression on the conscience of America. All over the country women vowed not to wear plumes on their hats. Many sent money to buy a home for Guy Bradley's widow and children. One of the strongest voices to be raised against the plume hunters was that of Theodore Roosevelt, the President of the United States. After Bradley's death he wrote to the Audubon Societies:

A roseate spoonbill prepares to catch fish with his long bill.

"Permit me on behalf of Mrs. Roosevelt and myself to say how heartily we sympathize with your efforts to stop the sale and use of the so-called 'aigrettes'—the plumes of the white herons."

With leaders such as this, the support for bird protection increased. Not long afterward New York passed a strong law that made it a crime to bring the plumes of most birds into the state. Since the milliners' factories were located in New York City, the law wiped out the market for plumes. There was no need to kill any more plume birds. New York passed this law just in time.

Many people had helped to rescue the birds before they disappeared from our country. But no one had played a more important part than Guy Bradley, who gave his life to put an end to a shameful business.

U.S. Department of the Interior

Roseate spoonbills are noted for their rose color and spoonlike bills.

PORTRAIT OF A PLUME BIRD

In Florida they called it the *pink curlew.*

In Louisiana they called it *pinkie.*

In South America they called it *garza rosada.*

In England, where the bird's feathers are white, they used to call it *spooney* or *banjo-bill.*

Today we call it the *roseate spoonbill.* The bird's name tells us what it looks like. It has beautiful rose-colored feathers, and it has a bill that is shaped something like a spoon. It is the most spectacular of the plume birds.

Surprisingly, the roseate spoonbill was not as highly prized by the plume hunters as some other birds. The bright rose of its feathers faded quickly. Yet no plume bird came closer to total destruction in this country than the roseate spoonbill.

It declined chiefly because it is so shy. When the hunters "shot out" rookeries of egrets and herons, the spoonbills were frightened from their nests. They did not come back to nest again. They stopped laying eggs and raising young.

Just before World War II the National Audubon Society asked an ornithologist to make a study of the roseate spoonbill. The ornithologist's name was Robert Porter Allen. He set up a "blind" in their rookeries and lived with the birds for sixteen months. His blind consisted of a small tent with peep-holes cut in its sides. In that way he was able to watch the birds but they were not able to see him.

It is possible to tell a lot about how a bird feeds and what it eats just by looking at it. The roseate spoonbill needs long legs because it feeds by wading through the water. It has a bill six inches long that it thrusts underwater to reach its food.

Its bill, however, is not used like a spoon. The water in which a spoonbill feeds is often so muddy that it cannot see the bottom. The bird swings its bill from side to side as it wades. Sensitive nerves at the end of this marvelous bill let the bird feel what it cannot see.

Instinct causes the roseate spoonbill to swing its bill from side to side while feeding. We know that this is so because scientists have watched these birds in captivity. When they approach food that has been left for them in a tray, they begin to swing their bills even though the food is not underwater. They also swing their bills back and forth when they get hungry.

When the spoonbill feels or sees something that it likes to eat—such as minnows, shrimps, fiddler crabs, or water insects—it seizes the animal with its bill. The tiny animal cannot escape because the bill is strong and it is two inches wide at the tip. Then the spoonbill tilts back its head and the animal slides into a pouch in the bird's throat. This pouch is much like a pelican's. Finally the spoonbill swallows whatever is in the pouch.

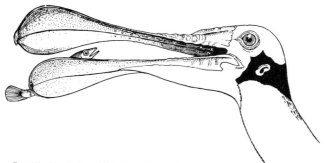

From *The Roseate Spoonbill* by Robert Porter Allen; courtesy of National Audubon Society

Tiny fish cannot escape from the spoonbill's strong beak.

Robert Allen also studied the breeding cycle of the roseate spoonbill. "I will not speak of 'Mr. and Mrs. Spoonbill,' or refer to their 'love' for each other," he wrote in his report. "It is much more complicated than that—and much more interesting."

A bird cannot "think" about doing something as we do. It acts in response to what is going on around it. For instance, during its breeding period a bird reacts to stimuli—to the movements, postures, and sounds of other birds. One activity leads to another. Unless the stimuli occur in a certain order, the bird may not go on to perform the next step in the "breeding cycle."

Allen learned that spoonbills do not stay with the same mates year after year. Each spring a spoonbill finds a new mate. The birds come together in rookeries to select their mates.

FIGURE 1: Much of the bird's early activity at the rookery can be explained by its excitement as the cycle starts. Many times each day the whole flock suddenly rises into the air and circles the rookery. Scientists call this an "up-flight." At other times the birds will stand in the shallow water together. If another spoonbill flies overhead, every bird in the group points its bill in the air and stares upward. This is called "sky gazing."

FIG. 1 "Sky gazing."

FIGURE 2: It is the female that chooses a mate. She "advertises" herself by standing on a branch high in a bush or a tree. Sometimes she takes a branch in her bill and shakes it. All the males who are interested in the female fly past, beating their wings. Each male tries to make a place for himself on the branch next to her. Finally she allows one male to land. Later he drives all other males away from his "territory." He also brings a stick to the female, shaking it in his bill. She accepts the stick, shakes it in her own bill, and then lays it among the branches at her feet. Nest building has started.

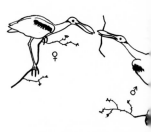

FIG. 2 The male brings the stick to the female.

FIGURE 3: The male continues to bring sticks, which the female uses to build the nest. Copulation takes place when the nest is nearly finished. The female stands on the

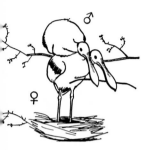

3 Both birds grasp the stick.

FIG. 4 A parent gives
the nest relief call.

nest, shaking a loose twig in her bill. The male reaches across her back so that he can grasp the same twig with his bill. Then they shake the twig together with short rapid movements of their heads. The female crouches on the nest. The male mounts her back and grasps her bill in his. Finally he hops off, and both preen their own feathers.

FIGURE 4: The female lays the first egg about a week later and then lays two to four more within a few days. The parents take turns sitting on the eggs to keep them warm. Sometimes one parent gets "bored" sitting on the eggs. When this happens it picks up twigs in its bill and plays with them. Then, if it wants its mate to take its place, it gives a "relief call"—low clucking sounds. The other bird comes to the nest. They rattle their bills together, and then the second bird takes over the job of sitting on the eggs.

The information that Robert Allen collected about the feeding and breeding habits of roseate spoonbills has helped to rescue them from extinction. Since Allen's famous study, their numbers have increased steadily in Florida. And today visitors to Everglades National Park can watch these marvelous wild birds flying and feeding in their natural habitat.

Figs. 1–4 from *The Roseate Spoonbill* by Robert Porter Allen; courtesy of National Audubon Society

Dennis Cowals—Black Star

Sea Otters

CHAPTER TWO

Dennis Cowals–Black Star

In Trouble–Again

Margaret Owings does Indian embroidery atop the cliffs at Big Sur.

Margaret Owings lives in a house built into the high cliffs at Big Sur on the California coast. On a porch that overlooks the Pacific Ocean she keeps binoculars and a high-powered navy-surplus telescope. Many times during the day she watches all sorts of rare and interesting wild creatures live out a drama far more exciting than any television program: migrating sea lions . . . whales . . . strange seabirds. But of all the creatures she watches, none are more fascinating or have a more poignant history than the sea otters.

"Not long ago word reached us that a baby otter had been washed up on the beach," Margaret Owings says. "A man who works for the state Fish and Game Department went down and brought the otter back in a box, wrapped in a blanket—the dearest baby animal I have ever had the opportunity to see. They thought he was about two weeks old. Rich coat of fur, tiny nub of black leather ear, tiny little eyes, and tiny little sounds. I have seen many baby animals, but never one to equal this one in utter charm."

Unfortunately, many dead sea otters are found washed up on the California beaches, too. They are adult otters, and their bodies bear bullet holes, knife wounds, and deep cuts left by the propellers of fishing boats.

Margaret Owings, like many other people along the California coast, was angered and upset by these killings. She saw them as a renewed threat to the uncertain existence of the sea otters.

Like the plume birds of the Everglades,

these creatures were once driven to the edge of extinction because of "high fashion." For the sea otter's rich, warm fur is considered one of the most precious in the world. The desire for otter skins was a principal reason for the exploration of the northern Pacific Ocean in the eighteenth century. The early Russian explorers were amazed at the numbers and the tameness of these valuable animals.

"They covered the shore in droves," one Russian traveler wrote. "They would come up to our fires and would not be driven away."

The skins of the sea otter were in great demand in China, Japan, and the capital cities of Europe. When she saw one of the beautiful skins, Catherine the Great, the empress of Russia, ordered a cloak of sea otter fur to cover her from her throat to her ankles. Soon hunters flocked to the shores and islands of the northern Pacific in search of the valuable otter skins.

At first the sea otters were so tame they could be killed with clubs. "When it receives a vigorous blow upon the head," a hunter wrote, "the otter falls upon the ground, covers its eyes with its paws, and keeps them so, no matter how many times it is struck."

Later they were hunted with nets and guns. Many hundreds of thousands were killed. Not even thick fogs protected the otters, for the hunters could detect them by listening for the cries of the young otters. The pups were not able to stay underwater very long. Each time the pup came to the surface its mother also came up to protect it. Often she ducked her pup's head underwater again to stifle its cries. Even when the hunters appeared, she would not leave her pup.

"It is very seldom that she will desert her young," a scientist wrote. "She almost always clings to it with the truest devotion to the last."

By the end of the nineteenth century many people believed that the sea otter was on the edge of extinction. A dead otter found in the Pribilof Islands in 1894 was the last of its kind there—though, when the islands were first discovered, two sailors had killed five thousand otters in less than a year!

Along the California coast, hunters from Mexico and the United States joined the Russians in slaughtering the sea otters. Finally, in 1911, the United States, Russia, and

Drawing by D. W. Ovenden 1967 Copyright © George Rainbird Ltd. 1969

The otter's webbed paws and streamlined body make him an excellent swimmer.

A mother otter holds her two-week-old pup on her chest.

Karl W. Kenyon

other nations signed a treaty to protect these animals. The hunters and furriers did not complain about the treaty because there were no longer enough sea otters left in the world to make hunting them worthwhile.

Here and there, in remote coves, small herds remained. Only a few people knew of their existence. Hidden from the outside world, the sea otters were able to raise their young and spend lazy days drifting and diving in the surf without fear of human hunters. Then, in 1938, the sea otter once more became a part of the California coast. A small herd of otters was sighted in a cove in the northern part of the state. To people who had believed that they would never see these charming animals, it was as if the sea otters had been called back from the dead. Under strict protection by the state, the otters gradually increased. They did not become plentiful, but biologists estimated that more than seven hundred of them lived along the California coast.

"We have twelve sea otters that live in the great beds of kelp, or seaweed, six hundred feet below our house," Margaret Owings says. "Sometimes we can't see them because they are searching for food underwater. But at other times we love to watch them while they rest or play on the rise and fall of the waves. A number of otters usually rest together. We call it a *raft* of otters. We see the mothers holding their babies on their chests, or perhaps one will have her pup's head resting on her feet and its body swung out over the water at a right angle."

Today the sea otters face a new enemy. Not long ago, many commercial fishermen claimed that the otters were eating too many abalones, which are a kind of shellfish much in demand in the California markets. The fishermen raised a cry: "The otters must go!"

Some abalone fishermen began to carry guns in their boats. Others turned to representatives in the state legislature, asking them to pass laws to help them get rid of the animals. The fishermen said that they could not make any money because the otters took the abalones off the rocks before they did. If people like Margaret Owings had not acted, California might have lost its sea otters once again.

When Margaret Owings was a child, the

A group of otters "raft" in a kelp bed.

animals she got to know—both in the woods and in her books—delighted her. She grew up on a hillside in Berkeley, California, in a place called Thousand Oaks.

"When I was a child our neighborhood was just as the name describes it," she says today. "It had lots of oak trees, lots of big rocks to climb, and lots of beautiful untouched natural areas to explore. We lived in a pretty house built on a rock with the trees and a garden all around. I spent most of my time outside. I used to leave my house by an upstairs window, swinging on a live oak branch to a rock that was twenty feet high. It was wonderful to have all the trees and wild flowers and animals as a part of my life."

On rainy days Mrs. Owings liked to take down her books and read about the animals that she saw in the woods around her. "My favorite was a book called *Lightfoot the Deer* by Thornton Burgess," she says. "I read it over and over. It was the greatest book in the world, I thought. And it made me associate my life with the lives of the animals."

But Margaret Owings also learned that everybody did not share her love for wild things. Some people were interested in animals only to kill them.

"I remember that one time I saw two boys pull down a blue jay's nest and begin shooting the young birds that were flapping about on the ground. They said they had been told that blue jays are bad because they rob other birds' nests. Actually, of course, blue jays play their part in the wild community just the way other birds do.

"I was so angry I wanted to strike them. I lifted my arm—and then I just made up my mind that I was going to do something about it. There are other ways to change things without hitting people. I suppose that the interests I have followed in my adult years find their roots in this little incident that offended me so brutally."

Even after she had grown up and was graduated from college, her feelings did not change. She married a famous architect named Nathaniel Owings, who shares her love for the natural world. He designed their beautiful home at Big Sur. There they are able to enjoy the broad expanse of sea and sky and the wild things they see every day—

like the red-tailed hawk that rides on the air currents *below* their windows.

For years Margaret Owings drew great pleasure from watching the sea otters and sea lions barking on the rocks below. Then one day she found, tucked away in the back pages of a newspaper, an article so small that she almost overlooked it. The article said that the state senate had passed a bill to "get rid of 75 percent of the sea lions along the California coast." This would be done by throwing sticks of dynamite into the sea lion herds. The reason for this was that commercial fishermen had complained that the sea lions were eating *their* salmon.

"I just couldn't believe it," she says. "It was late at night, I remember, and I began to cry. I could hear the two hundred fifty sea lions below our house barking and talking together. My husband came over to me, laid his hand on my shoulder, and said, 'It's going to be all right, Margaret. We'll work on it tomorrow.'"

Sea lions, of course, are the marvelous animals that circus people call seals. They are friendly and easy to tame, and are often taught to balance big rubber balls on the tips of their noses. When they perform their tricks they clap their flippers as enthusiastically as the audience applauds.

Margaret Owings realized that she had a responsibility and an opportunity to help these threatened animals. The experiences she gained in this struggle were to prove important afterward, when she set out in the more difficult struggle to save the sea otters.

"I realized I didn't have much time to save those sea lions," she says. "The state senate had already passed the bill, and the state assembly would vote on it soon. I'd never done anything like this on a large scale. I knew I would have to go before the legislators and testify about why those important and beautiful marine animals must be saved. No one else was doing anything about it. I was scared to death."

Margaret Owings went right to work. Because she did not know what course to follow, she hired a lobbyist—a man who would talk to the state legislators in the capitol building and get them to listen to the other side of the story.

"In the meantime, I found out all about the sea lions and their value to the state and the pleasure they give to people," she says. "I found out what they eat and I found that salmon are only a small part of their diet. Sea lions, I learned, eat a great many lamprey eels, which prey on the fish the fishermen were trying to catch for the market.

"I had 'fact sheets' printed with all this information in them. I mailed ten thousand fact sheets to people, asking them to write letters to the legislators. I sent stories and photographs of the sea lions to newspaper editors. Everything had to be done in a great hurry. It was like running General Motors from the end of my dining room table!"

Soon she found that some of the state legislators were listening to these facts with interest and sympathy. As a result, the bill was defeated. It was at this point that Mar-

Dennis Cowals—Black Star

An otter floats in the surf with its thick paws resting on its chest.

garet Owings learned some of the tricks that people use when they are trying to pass a bad law. The men who wanted to kill the sea lions realized that Margaret Owings stood in their way, so they decided to write a new bill for the legislature. This bill would permit them to kill the sea lions with dynamite everywhere along the California coast—except in the area near the Owings' home.

"Imagine!" she says. "They thought that if they left a few sea lions on our beach for us to watch, we would forget about all the others. Well, we just laughed and went right on fighting to save all the sea lions—and we won."

Margaret Owings had learned that by itself the love of animals and wild places will not save them when they are threatened with destruction. It is necessary to learn the facts about the problem and then act on them.

Her belief in direct action was strengthened by an incident that occurred later. The Owings sometimes saw a mountain lion in the canyon below their home at Big Sur, and its big footprints could be seen along their road and beside their mailbox. It made them happy to know that they lived close to such a wild and powerful creature.

But the state of California paid a bounty—a sum of money—to anyone who killed a mountain lion. One day Mrs. Owings opened the local newspaper and saw a picture of a grinning boy standing beside a mountain lion he had shot at Big Sur. She knew that she would never again see this magnificent animal moving gracefully along the stream of their canyon.

"I made up my mind that this mountain lion was not going to die in vain," she says.

She began a fight to remove the bounty on mountain lions. She asked help from scientists who knew the value of the mountain lion in the animal community. Again, she sent out fact sheets to thousands of people. With sound, scientific knowledge behind their arguments, Margaret Owings and the scientists persuaded the state legislators that the value of the lion is far greater than any minor damage it causes to ranchers. The legislators voted to remove the bounty.

Meanwhile, Margaret Owings continued to

study birds and marine life through the powerful telescope from her home on the cliffs. She saw many exciting events take place in the sea below.

"One day I was sitting on our porch sewing when I happened to look out across the water," she says. "Suddenly I saw the fins of killer whales cutting through the surface of the water. These creatures aren't really whales—they're large dolphins that are the fiercest of marine animals. I counted twelve of them. They were swimming swiftly toward the shoreline, two by two, heading straight for a herd of sea lions.

"I pointed my telescope toward the scene. I could see about sixty sea lions in the water apparently aware of the coming attack. They swam together in one solid, black circle and turned their heads toward the column of killer whales coming toward them. The killer whales kept coming, still two by two. When they reached the sea lions, they divided and encircled them, just like a troop of cavalry.

"The instant the two lines met it was as if someone gave a signal—because the killer whales all dived under the herd of sea lions! Then the sea lions went under, too.

"It seemed ages before I could see anything more. Finally a few of the killer whales shot up to the surface with sea lions in their mouths. The water was bubbling just as if it were boiling, and there was blood in the whitecaps. After that the sea lions didn't come back to our beach for a long time."

Margaret Owings knew that killer whales had been attacking sea lions and sea otters

A hungry otter cracks two cockles together to open their shells.

for thousands of years. They killed a few each time, of course, but they never threatened entire populations of the animals. Only when thoughtless human beings came on the scene, armed with high-powered rifles, dynamite, or deadly poisons, did wildlife face extinction.

In 1963, human beings once more threatened the sea otters along the California coast. Only a few years before, the state of California had set aside one hundred miles of that coast as a Sea Otter Refuge. Why were some people killing the otter even though it was a "protected animal"? Was the sea otter eating all the abalones? If so, how did it happen that the abalone industry was increasing its markets each year?

These were the questions that Margaret Owings asked, and she knew that unless they could be answered truthfully the sea otters were in trouble.

"The sea otters deserve better treatment than they've had at the hands of human beings," she told a friend. "Do you realize that *millions* of sea otters once swam and played along this coastline? Do you realize that these few delightful little animals have courageously come back only to be threatened again because they like abalones?"

Margaret Owings had made up her mind to see that these animals were given at least a fair chance to survive. To do so she set up a three-part strategy:

1. Let as many people as possible know about the sea otter and the dangers it faced.
2. Organize a group called Friends of the Sea Otter so that concerned people could work together.
3. Encourage scientific studies so that the struggle to protect the otters would be based on sound knowledge.

Margaret Owings, like most people who have watched sea otters closely, knew that their value could not be measured in dollars and cents. The California sea otters are too rare to be exhibited in zoos and aquariums. But the extension of modern life, in the form of new highways, has given hundreds of thousands of tourists an opportunity to watch the otters feeding and resting along the coast. A report published by the state of

California says: "Nearly all of the 30,000 annual visitors to the Morro Bay State Park Museum express an interest in sea otters. So do a majority of the 178,000 annual visitors to Point Lobos State Park, where sea otters are considered the greatest single attraction."

For Margaret Owings, so familiar with the sea otters and their world, they were the "greatest single attraction" along the coast.

With such appealing animals as her subject, it was not long before Margaret Owings was successfully reaching the public with the story of the sea otters and their way of life. Then she began to look into reports on the abalone industry.

As she started to put her information together, it became obvious that the growth of the abalone industry was a key factor in the problem. The shellfish were becoming more and more popular on restaurant menus. And for the first time the state was allowing abalones that were harvested off the California coast to be sold in other states. From 1947 to 1966, the number of licensed abalone fishermen in California had increased from 130 to 705. This last fact gave Margaret Owings a vital clue.

The number of men engaged in harvesting abalones had greatly increased in recent years, and the amount of shellfish taken had also increased each year. But, since there were more fishermen trying to gather abalones, each one found fewer than the individual fisherman had in 1947. The abalone fishermen, instead of blaming the growing number of men involved in their trade for the smaller harvests, began to blame the sea otters.

"The sea otters have to go!" the fishermen decided. "We can't make a living if the otters eat the abalones before we harvest them."

It seemed that the abalone fishermen had gained a head start in their war against the sea otters. People walking along the beaches began to find lifeless otters drifting in the surf, their thick, rich hides pierced by rifle bullets.

Margaret Owings once again began to write letters to state legislators and to newspaper editors, asking them for protective measures to guard the sea otters. "The sea otter needs a friend," she said. As planned, she organized a group of people called Friends of the Sea Otter. It was made up of men and women from all over the country who believed that the animals should not be condemned simply because a few men believed they were costing them money.

As a result of the efforts of Margaret Owings and the Friends of the Sea Otter, the state legislature asked the California Fish and Game Department to prepare a report on the otters and the special world they live in. The department carefully studied the hundred miles along the California coast where the otters live. It also held meetings to hear all sides of the dispute and gather information. Margaret Owings attended these meetings. So did scientists, members of the abalone industry, and officials of the Fish and Game Department.

"The abalone fishermen themselves attended with their wives, their divers, and their boatmen," she says. "They dragged in large boxes of abalone shells that bore holes in them the size of silver dollars. These shells, they pointed out, were abalones eaten by otters. They did *not* haul in the tons of shells that were harvested by the fishermen.

"But we all learned a great deal. We learned that the sea otters were just holding their own along the coast. The most recent counts showed that there were now about one thousand otters. This doesn't mean that they were increasing [an earlier estimate had put the number at seven hundred]—just that we had better methods of counting them and had included all of them in the count.

James A. Mattison

"Why weren't the sea otters increasing as fast as they should? We heard biologists say that the bodies of sea otters were being found washed up on shore. Some of them had been shot or stabbed.

"The fishermen who came to the meetings were angry about the presence of sea otters near the abalone areas. They wanted the state to remove them. The fishermen said they would take the matter into their own hands—meaning they would kill the otters," Margaret Owings says. "I reminded them that some otters had already been found dead.

" 'I know, I know,' one of the fishermen said to me. 'You think that we're killing the otters. Well, maybe so. But I want to tell you it's mighty hard to shoot an otter from a rocking boat.'

A mother otter often wraps her babies in kelp to prevent them from floating away while she searches for food.

"Then some other fishermen joined in and began to argue about the best way to shoot an otter so that it would sink and not leave any telltale traces."

Margaret Owings and the other Friends of the Sea Otter knew that they must come to some agreement soon with the state. If they did not, the otters in commercial fishing areas would be killed. At last the Fish and Game Department's report was ready, and it told much about the sea otter and how it lives. The report drew a complicated picture, showing that there was more involved in the dispute than simply sea otters and abalones.

Kelp, a long, tough seaweed that grows in thick beds off the California coast, is an important part of the picture. It forms the "forest" in which both the sea otters and the

abalones live. Two kinds of kelp are important to man because they are harvested by
companies that produce a substance called
algin, which is used in many industrial pro-
cesses.

Kelp is also important to many creatures
of the sea. They are born in the great kelp
beds, they find shelter there, and they use
the kelp itself for food. California protects
the kelp beds. Harvesters must be licensed,
and their take is limited by the Fish and
Game Department.

One of the sea animals that is dependent
on kelp is the abalone. There are many kinds
of abalones living off the California coast,
but the most important are red abalones and
pink abalones. These creatures feed on kelp.
In 1957 the temperature of the water rose off
the coast of California. The kelp, which cannot stand high temperatures, disappeared.
Many of the abalones disappeared, too.
Others stopped growing, and their meat became shrunken and watery. When the water
became colder again in 1960, the kelp and the
abalones returned.

Almost sixty percent of all the red abalones taken each year in California are harvested in Morro Bay. Fishermen using boats
specially equipped for underwater work dive
for the abalones and pry them off the rocky
sea bottom where they live among the kelp
beds. In a recent year, fishermen sold
1,775,000 pounds of abalone meat to whole-
salers at $2.40 a pound.

Another creature that feeds on kelp is the
sea urchin, which looks like a little ball with

short needles sticking out of it. A bather who steps on one at the shore is likely to get a painfully punctured foot. There is little demand for sea urchins as food for human beings, so their numbers are not kept down by the fishermen.

Sea urchins usually move out of an area after they have eaten most of the kelp beds. This gives the kelp a chance to recover. But now scientists have learned that sea urchins can go on living in an area even after most of the kelp has been eaten. The reason for this is that sea urchins also gain nourishment from polluted water. Much of California's offshore water is polluted by sewage. So the sea urchins stay on, completely destroying kelp beds that otherwise would be harvested by man for industry or used as food by other sea animals such as abalones.

The Fish and Game Department's report went on to point out that, although the number of sea otters off the California coast had not increased in recent years, they had extended their range. In 1957 fishermen noticed a sharp dip in their abalone harvest at North Morro Bay. They also noticed that sea otters were moving into the area. So they blamed the sea otter for the scarcity of abalones.

But the story is not so simple, for that was also the year when the water temperature rose in that area. The kelp beds shrank, and the abalones had nothing to eat. Only when the temperature dropped once more did the kelp have a chance to recover and provide food for the abalones.

Otters help to protect kelp beds by eating spiny sea urchins.

The scientists who prepared the report believed that if the otters had not come into the area the abalones might not have returned to their former numbers. The otters ate some of the abalones, of course. But they also ate many of the sea urchins that might have kept the kelp beds from growing again.

"It seems likely that, in the period when otters were absent from the Central California coastline, sea urchins limited the growth of kelp," says the Fish and Game Department's report. "By reducing the numbers of sea urchins, which feed on the kelp, otters could facilitate development of the kelp beds—which in turn provide more food for abalones."

This important report would not have been prepared if Margaret Owings and her friends had not come to the sea otter's defense. Using the facts provided by the report, both sides were able to talk over the problem. It was clear now that the sea otters, although they liked to eat abalones, were not as harmful as the fishermen said they were. In fact, as we have seen, they actually *helped* the abalones.

But the report said that in some abalone-fishing areas there might be too many sea otters. Margaret Owings and other concerned people realized that if action were not taken in those areas, the sea otters might be killed by throwing "seal bombs" into their midst. So she agreed to the state's plan to trap a total of twenty-four otters in big nets and transport them away from the areas where they were in danger. The state agreed to take care not to harm the otters while they were being moved.

The lives of the sea otters had been saved, at least for the moment. But Margaret Owings knew that the animals were in constant need of watchful attention. She would not stop trying to protect them.

So she and the other Friends of the Sea Otters have become "otter watchers." They use binoculars and telescopes to keep track of them from the shore. They count the otters, keep a record of their activities, and try to find out what kinds of food they eat. The information that they collect is turned over to scientists who are now making an even closer study of sea otters.

"I place this little animal high on my list of special values," Margaret Owings says. "The return of the otter to our coastal waters is an important event in the total picture of our sea life. And remember—the sea otter gives thousands of people a rare pleasure."

THE SEA OTTER—
MADE FOR ITS WORLD

On days when the sun is bright, Margaret Owings likes to point her big navy telescope toward the shifting tides where the otters move like dark shadows through the foam. She focuses the telescope on one of the sea otters, revealing a very streamlined animal, despite its thick neck and short legs. Its heavily muscled body swells in a graceful curve that runs from its head and neck all the way down to its broad hips.

The sea otter is perfectly made for the world in which it lives. Its remarkable body always reminds Margaret Owings of a contortionist. A sea otter's skin hangs so loosely on its body that, if she held it firmly by the back of its neck, it could still twist its head around to bite her hand. And inside that loose skin the otter's body is able to twist and bend almost as if it were boneless. Though it has a skeleton like other animals, an otter is able to touch its nose to its tail by bending forward or backward.

The sea otter's flexible body also helps to propel it through the water, and its feet are webbed so that it can use them as paddles. When swimming, the otter bends its head and tail toward one another and then unbends them, much as a fish swims by flexing its body from side to side.

The sea otter's fur, dark, thick, and tipped with silvery gold, makes a perfect raincoat. Water is repelled by the long outer "guard hairs." Beneath them is an undercoat of very fine hairs so dense that they insulate the otter against both heat and cold.

"Sometimes, after I've been writing letters and licking stamps and attending meetings, I grow tired," Margaret Owings says. "And I wonder if all this work to save the sea otters is really worth it. Then I come out here on the terrace and watch them feeding and playing, and I know that I'm being rewarded by the otters themselves."

A sea otter must be a good diver because the shellfish it eats are found on the bottom of the sea. It can dive as deep as 350 feet and remain active underwater for several minutes. It is helped to do this by a process that scientists call *bradycardia*. A muscle above the sea otter's diaphragm acts to slow down its pulse. This lowers the rate at which oxygen is taken from its bloodstream. Thus the sea otter does not have to come up for air as quickly as other mammals do.

When Margaret Owings looks for the otters in the morning and there are none in sight, she knows that they are beneath the surface, looking for mussels, scallops, abalones, starfish, snails, sea urchins, and other shellfish. As she watches, the surface of the water may break suddenly and a large male otter may appear. Margaret Owings can see through her telescope that the creature carries two objects in its paws.

The otter rolls on its back. First it places on its chest a heavy stone that it has carried up from the sea bottom. Then it takes the shellfish—perhaps an abalone—in its paws and begins to pound it with short, sharp

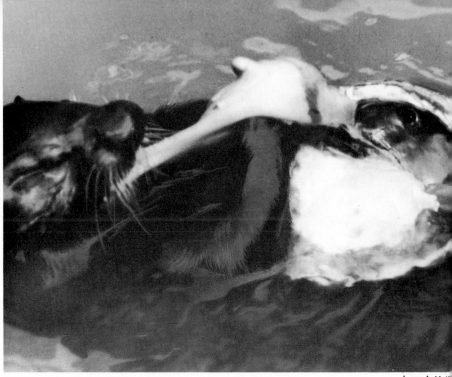
James A. Matt

An otter pulls a red abalone out of its shell.

strokes on the stone. The shell breaks open
at last. Lifting the broken shell to its mouth
as if it were a bowl, the otter begins to feed
on the meat inside. The sea otter is one of
the few animals in the world that uses a tool
to get at its meal.

The big sea otter has finished eating now.
Margaret Owings watches it as it rests, drifting lazily in the surf. But there is more to
come. Moving quickly and quietly through
the water nearby is a young otter. There is
no more playful animal than an otter, and
the young ones delight in teasing their elders.
The youngster comes up under the old male,
tugs at its tail, and pulls it under. Sputtering,
the old male turns on its tormentor. But the
young otter swims swiftly away, propelled
through the water by its webbed paws and
its flexible, streamlined body.

Crabs are also part of the sea otter's diet.

Most fun of all to watch are the baby otters, or pups. They're never far from their mothers. If the mother is ready to dive for food, she often wraps her pup in long streams of kelp. If the pup falls asleep, the kelp wrapped around its tiny body will keep it from floating away in the shifting tides. Whenever the mother returns to the surface of the water, she swims over to her pup to make certain it has not twisted loose.

But Margaret Owings notices that, for the most part, the pup remains with its mother wherever she goes. If she dives below the surface, the adolescent pup tries to dive, too. And when they're resting together the mother otter rolls the pup onto her chest and holds it in her strong paws. The pup, perhaps lulled by the rise and fall of the surf, soon falls asleep, its head on its mother's chest.

CHAPTER THREE

A Wild Corner of the City

Mary M. Thacher

Despite its nearness to the city, the Jamaica Bay Wildlife Refuge provides a haven for birds and bird watchers alike.

Herbert Johnson, his wife, and his daughter are very special people. Like eight million others, they live in the great city of New York. Most New Yorkers cannot do anything about the smelly buses and trucks that clatter past their homes and apartments. Nor can they change the view through their windows in sections of the city where mailboxes and trash baskets outnumber trees.

But the Johnsons have a different view of the city. Where they live, rugosa rose, chokecherry, autumn olive, and other shrubs and trees grow in abundance. Instead of noisy trucks and buses, they are more likely to watch the comings and goings of some of the most fascinating birds in North America—the great blue heron, the glossy ibis, the short-eared owl, the snowy egret, the common gallinule, the pied-billed grebe, the hooded merganser, the snow goose, the black skimmer.

The Johnsons do not live in a zoo, however. They live in a wild corner of New York

Rafael Macia

City that has been created, for the most part, by Herbert Johnson himself. It is called the Jamaica Bay Wildlife Refuge.

Most New Yorkers do not even know that this wildlife refuge exists. Jamaica Bay is a large body of water, eight miles long and nearly four miles wide. It lies between New York City's boroughs of Brooklyn and Queens. The bay was formed about ten thousand years ago, when streams from the melting glaciers that covered the region began to flow into the Atlantic Ocean. The streams dropped their loads of sand, forming beaches just offshore. Over the centuries these beaches developed into barriers that protect the bay and its small islands from the open ocean.

For thousands of years, then, this rich area of grassy islands and salt marshes has served as a breeding place for marine life. Fish and shellfish prospered in the bay. Seabirds of all kinds came to feed on the variety of life. But when New York began to grow, the bay began to suffer. Man poured his wastes into its water and dredged huge amounts of sand from its bottom for his own uses. Thus Jamaica Bay has become one of the most polluted regions of the great city.

Today man's presence in Jamaica Bay is most obvious at John F. Kennedy International Airport. This airport, one of the most

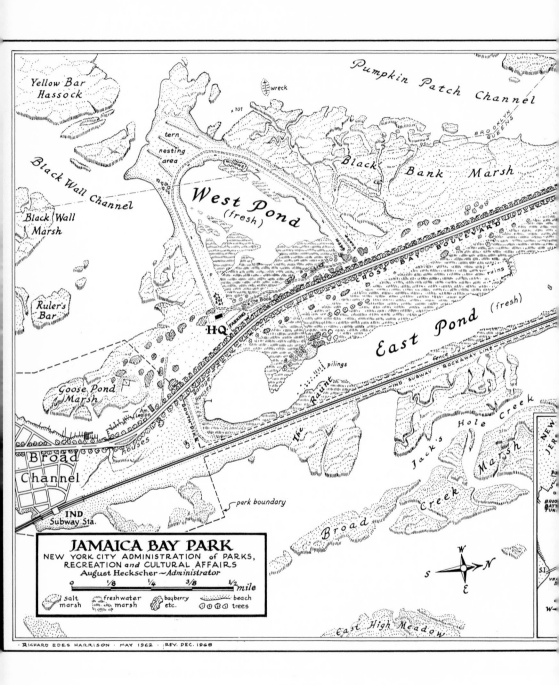

Yellow Bar
Hassock

wreck

Pumpkin Patch Channel

tern
nesting
area

BROOKLYN
QUEENS

Black Bank Marsh

Black Wall Channel

Willow

West Pond
(fresh)

Black Wall
Marsh

Ruler's
Bar

CROSS BAY BOULEVARD

ruins

HQ

PARKING

The Raunt

pilings

East Pond (fresh)

IND SUBWAY ROCKAWAY LINE

fence

Goose Pond
Marsh

Legion

SOUTH DIKE

barge
houses

Jack's Hole Creek

NEW JER

BROO
BATT
TUN

Broad
Channel

houses

park boundary

Creek Marsh

S.I.

IND
Subway Sta.

Broad Creek

JAMAICA BAY PARK
NEW YORK CITY ADMINISTRATION of PARKS,
RECREATION *and* CULTURAL AFFAIRS
August Heckscher ~ Administrator

0   ⅛   ¼   ⅜   ½
mile

salt
marsh

freshwater
marsh

bayberry
etc.

beach

trees

W
N
S
E

East High Meadow

· RICHARD EDES HARRISON · MAY 1962 · REV. DEC. 1968 ·

important in the world, was built on the edge of the bay. Parts of the bay were filled in so that the huge runways could be extended. Now the deafening noise of jet airliners is added to the pollution and the shoreline building projects that threaten to overwhelm this fragile piece of land.

Yet the bay's wildlife refuge and its flocks of marvelous birds have managed to withstand the threats of a modern city. Some people have called this a little miracle. But the people who know best say that the refuge and the birds are still there mostly because of the intelligence and hard work of one man—Herbert Johnson, the superintendent of the Jamaica Bay Wildlife Refuge.

Who ever heard of going to a wildlife refuge on the subway? A park, perhaps, or a zoo. But a wildlife refuge? Yet that is how thousands of New Yorkers find their way each year to Jamaica Bay. Many drive there, of course. A road has been built on a causeway from the part of Long Island called Queens through the small islands of Jamaica Bay. It is called Cross Bay Boulevard. The map on page 66 shows a subway track running south through the bay, not far from the boulevard. There is a subway station on an island called Broad Channel. Visitors get off at Broad Channel and walk back along the boulevard. Finally they come to the refuge—and Herbert Johnson.

Herbert Johnson is often found near the parking lot. Perhaps he is giving orders to the men who work under him, or sitting in a pickup truck that belongs to the Parks Department of New York City. He is a pleasant man, eager to answer visitors' questions. He is proud of the refuge that he and his men have built from almost nothing. There is enthusiasm in his voice as he points out the many living things, both plants and animals, that thrive in the refuge.

On a clear, cold morning in December not long ago, a visitor joined Herbert Johnson in the cab of his pickup truck. Johnson handed him a map of the refuge. Then he turned the truck out of the parking lot and drove past the refuge headquarters on the road that circles West Pond.

"We're beginning our tour of the refuge right here where it says 'HQ' on your map," Johnson said. "See, the dotted line that goes around West Pond is the roadway. Most of the people who come here walk around it, because we don't allow automobiles in here. But I use this truck to make inspection tours—to see that everything is all right."

Long lines of ducks flew across the sky. Many came in low to land with a splash on West Pond. It is a freshwater pond, surrounded by dikes that keep out the salt water of the bay. Beyond the pond are marshes of long grass and open patches of water leading into the bay. With the flying ducks, the marshes, and the open water, the Jamaica Bay Wildlife Refuge looks very much like a refuge in some remote part of the country.

But when the visitor looked beyond the marsh and the bay, there was the outline of New York's skyscrapers. The Empire State Building was clearly visible in the clear light

Mary M. Thacher

of morning. And behind him, across the small body of fresh water called East Pond, the visitor could see a large airliner, trailing its jet stream, rising from Kennedy Airport.

As the truck moved along the roadway, Herbert Johnson pointed toward the high grass that grew near the pond. The grass is called *Phragmites*—or giant reed. It is very tall, sometimes eight to ten feet in height. Phragmites used to be a rare plant in cities, but it spreads rapidly and is common near cities now. Where it grows in dense stands, as in Jamaica Bay, it looks impressive because of the long plumes at the top of each stalk. But many people consider it a nuisance.

"Phragmites used to grow all the way up to the path, so that you couldn't even see the pond from here," Johnson said. "Then we began to control it with the mowing machine. I know it doesn't have any food value, but we like to have some of it around because it grows very thickly and the ducks like to nest in it. Every plant has value."

The truck passed a group of men, women, and children walking along the path. They were carrying binoculars and small telescopes so that they would be able to see the birds more clearly. Some older people were sitting on wooden benches along the path, staring at ducks and geese on the mud flats.

"Those benches are like a lot of other things around here," Johnson said. "The city gives us very little money for equipment, so we have to go out and find what we need. The benches are made out of light poles that have been knocked down by cars on the parkways."

"What are those birds out there on the mud flats?" Johnson's visitor asked.

"Mostly brant," Johnson said. "They're a kind of small goose, with a black head and neck and a white rump. They normally feed

Mary M. Thacher

on eelgrass. In the 1930s a disease wiped out the eelgrass. Many of the brant starved to death. But now a lot of brant have changed their eating habits. They feed on sea lettuce, which grows around here, and they're doing fine.''

Johnson and his visitor were reaching the first curve in the road.

"Terns and skimmers nest here," Johnson said. "People have a lot of fun walking by here when those birds are nesting. The terns have forked tails. They're very graceful flyers. Some people call them sea swallows. And the skimmers have an interesting bill. The lower part is much longer than the upper part. They fly close to the water with their bills open. That long, lower part of the bill cuts the water and acts like a scoop for picking up little fish."

Johnson pointed out over the marshes.

"Look, there's a marsh hawk," he said. "It's got a big white patch on its rump. We've got a number of birds of prey out here. A peregrine falcon arrives here each winter and stays with us until spring. And we're expecting a snowy owl to show up anytime now."

Looking across the pond now into the tangle of Phragmites, the visitor saw a tall wading bird.

"That looks like one of the plume birds we see in the Everglades," he told Johnson.

A marsh hawk prepares to land.

"That's a glossy ibis," Johnson said. "They nest here now. I don't know why this one is staying around here so late in the year. If he can fly to Florida so easily, why does he stay here? I guess he's got a low IQ."

"Have you got herons and egrets nesting out here?"

Johnson nodded. "Yes, we've got lots of

common egrets and snowy egrets nesting in the summer. Plenty of black-crowned night herons, too. They're our worst predator. A predator is a bird or an animal that eats other birds or animals. The night herons eat a tremendous number of ducklings. They're a real menace."

"Have you got any other predators?"

"Not anything serious," Johnson said. "Oh, once in a while a cat gets in here. We have to trap it and send it to the Society for the Prevention of Cruelty to Animals. If it stayed around it would eat up a lot of small birds."

Johnson shook his head and laughed.

"I was driving around here one day when I spotted a cat," he said. "I jumped out of the truck and started to chase it. But I stumbled over a log. When I fell I put my hand down on the ground to stop myself. Luckily I had it cupped like this, because my hand went right over a rail. A rail is a little bird that hangs around in the tall grass. We don't see it very often. My hand cupped right over it. The rail scooted out and disappeared in the grass. I don't know who was more surprised—the rail or me!"

Johnson and his visitor drove toward Cross Bay Boulevard. West Pond was on their right, and Black Bank Marsh was on their left. A small bird ran across the path.

"That's a bobwhite," Johnson said. "The state gave us fifty pairs of them a few years ago, and now they've increased like anything. They're all over the refuge. They give people a lot of pleasure—especially when they call 'bob-*white!*'"

Virginia rail.

"Do you put out feed for them?"

"We're going to start putting out feed for them this week," Johnson said. "Up until December there's still plenty of seed around for them to eat."

The truck had reached another turn. As Johnson headed it back toward headquarters, the visitor could see the broad boulevard now.

"Do many birds get run over out on the boulevard?"

"We lose a few," Johnson said. "Especially in the early summer when the ducks finish nesting. When a mother duck finishes hatching out her young, for some reason she feels that she's got to take them to the other side of the boulevard. She'll walk them across the road, the little ducks strung out behind her. You'll hear brakes screeching out there. And then the little ones can't jump the curb and there's an awful lot of excitement going on."

As they neared headquarters, Johnson pointed to the small trees along the path.

"Those are called autumn olive," he said. "I had seen them growing along the state parkways a few years ago. The state planted them because they look nice. I noticed that birds and wildlife liked to eat the big red berries. So I planted some autumn olive here. I've been told by state officials that I was the first to plant many of these trees for wildlife. And they've done very well here. They attract lots of birds. During a severe winter I've even noticed muskrats sitting three or four feet up in the autumn olives eating the berries!"

Muskrat.

The visitor noticed "the book," which is kept in a box near the path. There is a pencil beside it. Visitors to the refuge may write down the date and the kinds of birds they have seen.

"Sometimes people fool around and say they've seen an ostrich or something like that," Johnson said smiling. "But most of the people are serious about bird watching, and 'the book' helps us to keep track of what we have here."

The tour was over. Afterward, Johnson and his visitor drove along Cross Bay Boulevard to the Superintendent's House. This is where the Johnson family lives. And this is where the visitor, looking over maps and newspaper clippings, learned about the difficult struggle to create the Jamaica Bay Wildlife Refuge.

Herbert Johnson was born on Long Island. His father was the superintendent of a large estate that was once owned by a wealthy man. While young Herbert was growing up, his father taught him many things about plants and how to grow them. The boy made up his mind he was going to become a *horticulturist*—a person who practices the science of growing plants. When Johnson finished school he worked for a while on an estate on Long Island. Then he joined the New York City Parks Department as a horticulturist.

"My job was to operate a soil-testing laboratory," Johnson said. "We were trying to develop special grasses for the city's public golf courses. The golfers wanted us to find

Bird watcher-Rafael Macia
Terns-Luther Goldman, Bureau of Sport Fisheries and Wildlife

Abandoned cars in the Jamaica Bay area contrast sharply with the beaut

a tough kind of grass so they wouldn't chop it up so badly with their clubs. I didn't know much about birds then. I was interested in birds mostly for their economic value because they eat a lot of bugs that otherwise might kill trees and shrubs."

Herbert Johnson might still be working in a laboratory if a number of people had not

of the adjoining refuge.

protested about the way the city was filling in marshes. Once there had been a number of marshy areas in New York. But many city officials didn't care whether or not a marsh or a swamp was a wonderful place for wildlife. They tended to think of a marsh only as a place that could be filled in with soil so that houses or roads could be built.

81

Like many big cities, New York seldom goes out of its way to make room for the natural world. For a long while hawks, foxes, and raccoons managed to find a place for themselves among the growing number of apartment houses and office buildings. But now most of these creatures' old homes have been wiped out by steel and concrete. The animals that a New Yorker is likely to see are either kept on a leash or manage to grub a living—as pigeons, rats, sparrows, squirrels, and gulls do—by taking what man throws away.

But in 1953 many people asked the city officials to spare some marshland as a haven for wildlife. The city officials agreed and set aside a small part of Jamaica Bay. They also pumped a great deal of sand out of the bay and used it to build the dikes that now surround the two ponds at the refuge. Then they gave Herbert Johnson the difficult job of creating a spot that would attract wildlife.

When Johnson arrived in Jamaica Bay it was not a very attractive place. The water in the bay was dirty. There was food—clams, mussels, and sea lettuce—for some of the ducks and shorebirds, but the area around the ponds had none of the plants that other birds need for food and shelter. For many species there was no reason to come to Jamaica Bay.

But Johnson knew that wild creatures will do well in the city if they are given a chance. People who like to watch wild birds often go to the city's few parks during the spring and fall, when birds are migrating. They know that they will see large numbers because there is food and shelter for them there.

Other city dwellers plant trees and shrubs in their tiny backyards to attract birds. One man who lives in the heart of Manhattan has seen over one hundred different kinds of birds in his tiny backyard. Among them was a woodcock. This chubby bird with a Pinocchio-like nose is eagerly sought by hunters and their dogs in the deep woods.

Woodcock.

So Johnson made up his mind to turn this part of Jamaica Bay into a place that birds would like.

"I didn't know too much about birds and other wildlife," Johnson said. "So I traveled around, visiting refuges and talking to wildlife biologists. I also read a lot of books about birds. Then I began to plant things that would attract wildlife. That isn't as easy as it sounds. I was a horticulturist, and I was used to planting everything in a very formal setting. It was hard for me to try to make the place look wild."

Johnson's first job was to plant beach grass to hold the sand in place so that the dikes would not blow away. But city officials gave Johnson very little help. He was forced to adapt an old mechanical cabbage planter so that it could be used to plant the grass.

"There was a lot of beach grass growing around the bay," Johnson said. "We went out and dug it up and planted it on the dikes. To give you some idea how much we planted, if we put all the rows of beach grass end to end, we'd have a row stretching all the way from here to Boston—almost two hundred fifty miles! But we didn't lose a grain of sand."

Once Johnson had "tied down" the sand with grass, he looked around for plants that would attract wildlife. He was limited in what plants he could use by the nature of the land and the climate. Most plants will not do well in Jamaica Bay. The soil is very sandy. The climate is hot and dry in the summer, and cold and windy in the winter.

Horst Schafer—Photo Trends

Johnson believed that Japanese black pine would grow well there. But the city officials would not give him any money to buy young trees. So Johnson, on his day off, went to a beach where Japanese black pines grew. He picked up all the pine cones he could find and took them back to Jamaica Bay.

"We took the seeds out of the cones and started them growing in a frame," Johnson said. "Then, when they'd grown into trees about a foot high, we planted them around the refuge. The trees are doing fine now. They're just at the age when they're developing their own cones, and lots of birds like grosbeaks come to feed on them."

Johnson also planted chokecherry, rugosa rose, autumn olive, and other shrubs and trees. Often he had to guess what plants would do well in Jamaica Bay and also attract birds. There was no one to teach him.

"It seems to me that a farm boy could do this job as well as a trained biologist—if the boy was observant," Johnson said. "Many times all I had to go on was my observation. I'd see a certain bush, and I'd see that a certain bird liked to feed on it. So I'd plant more of that kind."

The birds themselves proved that Johnson was right. Since Johnson began his planting, 305 different species of birds have been seen at the refuge. Fifty-five species have stayed there to nest. Robins, warblers, and many other species that were never seen at the refuge some years ago are now there in large numbers. Some very rare birds have visited the refuge, too.

The spur-winged ʃ

Vertical text on right side of image: M. S. Sopher–National Audubon Society

med for the tiny spur that protudes from under its wing.

"We've had a bird from Scandinavia—a red-winged thrush," Johnson said. "And we had an African bird, the spur-winged plover. But it turned out that the plover was really a bird that had escaped from a nature center in Stamford, Connecticut. And to top off the story, the bird had been born in the Bronx Zoo here in New York! So we don't claim much credit for that one."

Johnson also wanted to encourage more ducks, geese, and shorebirds to come to the refuge, so he put aquatic plants in the ponds. In the winter he spread corn for the ducks to feed on, and cut holes in the ice when the ponds became frozen over.

Under Herbert Johnson, the Jamaica Bay Wildlife Refuge has become a pleasant place for people, as well as for birds. His daughter, Christine, first came to the refuge as a child and grew up there surrounded by birds and plants. Now she goes to Manhattan Community College. None of the other city girls in her class have had Christine's experience with wild creatures.

Herbert Johnson believes that he has chosen the most wonderful career in the world.

"A lot of mothers call me," Johnson said, "and tell me that their child is interested in a career in wildlife management or conservation. They ask my advice about whether or not their child should go in for it. So I tell them that they couldn't have a better life. No one is going to get rich in this business, but they'll get a lot of satisfaction. Anyone who goes in for working with wildlife and preserving wild areas will have a wonderful life—and be doing something important, too."

But Johnson continues to have many problems in his work. He must patrol the refuge constantly. Along with the cats that stray in and eat the nesting birds, thieves come in at night to chop down the Japanese pines to use as Christmas trees. And once in a while a hunter tries to shoot birds in the refuge.

D. Cruikshank—National Audubon Society

A mother robin and her young.

Johnson points out that there is also danger from other city officials:

"A lot of these people look at the refuge and say, 'Oh, that place is no good to anyone. It's just a marsh.' The people from the Sanitation Department wanted to dump their garbage here. And other people have wanted to come out here and build restaurants or ball fields. But we have many friends, and they help us to get these ideas voted down."

Johnson's greatest problem is Kennedy Airport. That, he knows, is in Jamaica Bay

Herbert Johnson accompanies a group of bird watchers as a jet takes off from nearby Kennedy Airport.

to stay. So far, the roar of the huge jets landing and taking off from Kennedy Airport has not affected the birds. They don't seem to mind the noise. But many people say that the airport is not big enough to handle all of the air traffic and want to build longer runways for the planes. These new runways would have to be built on the finest feeding grounds of the ducks and shorebirds. And so civilization threatens to take away even this small wild corner of the city.

But Johnson has faith that the refuge is valuable enough to New York to be preserved. People in the city need a place where they can go and acquaint themselves with wild things. By proper planning, New York can keep both an airport and a thriving wild life refuge in Jamaica Bay.

"People come here from all over the country—and from all over the world, too," Johnson said. "They get off a plane at Kennedy Airport and come right over to see birds they've never had a chance to see anyplace else. Of course, we get some funny people here sometimes. They'll drive past on the boulevard and see the sign and come in wanting to know what it's all about.

" 'Birds?' they say. 'Where are the cages?' "

Many students in colleges, high schools, and grade schools are brought to the refuge by their teachers. Johnson likes to see them come. He believes that city youngsters, once they have had a chance to see beautiful creatures in the wild, will someday want to help rescue them, too.

"I remember one boy who came out here with his class," Johnson said. "I asked him how he liked it and he said he liked it fine. In fact, the next week he was out here by himself. He told me that while he was eating breakfast that morning his father was teasing him about being a bird watcher."

Johnson laughed as he recalled the story.

"Well, do you know that the next weekend the boy came out here again and brought his father. His father got so interested in watching birds that he bought binoculars and bird guides for both himself and his son. Now they come out here together all the time."

When things like that happen, Herbert Johnson feels that the refuge will survive. The people of New York City, he says, will help him to rescue the little wild corner that is left to them.

Binoculars and telescopes help visitors to see the birds in closer detail.

Children inspect pictures of birds that may be seen at the refuge.

VISITING A WILDLIFE REFUGE

What to Bring:

To get the most out of a visit to a wildlife refuge, it is best to bring binoculars in order to see the birds and other animals at close range. There are many guidebooks available that help visitors to learn the names of the wildlife and plants in the area. If possible, visitors should bring cameras to record what they see.

How to Look at Wild Birds:

When trying to identify a bird there are certain things to look for:

Is it large or small?

Does it usually fly alone or in a flock?

Does it eat on land, on water, or in the air?

Does it have any special markings?

The bird pictured here is a Canada goose. There are a number of things that can be said about this bird after watching it closely.

It is a large bird with a long neck.

It usually flies in a V-shaped flock.

It likes grain, so it usually eats on land.

Its long neck has special markings—a black "stocking" the length of the neck—and there is a white patch on its cheek.

How to Get to the Jamaica Bay Wildlife Refuge from the New York City Area:

BY CAR: Take the Shore Parkway, Southern Parkway, or Woodhaven Boulevard to Cross Bay Boulevard. Drive south on the boulevard one and one-half miles to the refuge.

BY SUBWAY: Take the Independent (IND) subway, trains "A," "E," or "HH," serving

Canada goose.

the Rockaways. Get off at Broad Channel station, walk west to Cross Bay Boulevard, then north ¾ of a mile to the refuge.

Entrance to the Jamaica Bay Wildlife Refuge is free, but a permit is required. To obtain a free permit write to:

Administration of Parks, Recreation and Cultural Affairs
The Arsenal
830 Fifth Avenue
New York, N.Y. 10021

CHAPTER FOUR

Man of Action

ISPA

ISPA

Natives recruited by John Walsh ride through the jungle in a dugout canoe.

A long, narrow boat, pointed at both ends and driven by an outboard motor, roared noisily through a dying South American jungle. There were three men in the boat. Two of them were darkskinned *Bush Negroes*—descendants of slaves who had been freed or escaped to the jungle more than one hundred years before. In the middle of the boat, which was called a "dugout," sat a tall, dark-haired American named John Walsh. His eyes continually searched the lifeless trees and vines overhead.

But it was one of the Bush Negroes who saw the tiny figure on a vine.

"Gwamba!" he called to Walsh, pointing upward.

Walsh saw the animal climbing slowly up the vine. He ordered the man tending the motor to turn in that direction. When they reached the vine, Walsh tugged at it. The vine, dead leaves, pieces of bark, and the tiny animal came tumbling into the water beside the boat. One of the men scooped the animal from the water with a net. He handed it to Walsh, who set the creature on a seat.

The three men looked at it. Though Walsh had seen pictures of it before, he had never seen this strange creature in the flesh. It was only eight inches long, with golden, silky fur, tiny eyes, and a long, pointed face.

"It's a pygmy anteater," Walsh told the other men. They had never even heard of the animal, though they had lived in the jungle all of their lives.

The anteater stared back at Walsh and sneezed. Laughing, Walsh picked up the tiny animal, knowing that an anteater has no teeth and could not bite him. The anteater wrapped its tail around Walsh's fingers and stood up. When it lifted its front paws, Walsh saw the two large claws on each paw. Later he remembered thinking that the anteater, with its paws up in front of its long nose, looked comically solemn, as if it were going to say its prayers.

Walsh was not prepared for what happened next. The anteater leaned forward and brought both of its paws downward, like a man chopping wood. The heavy claws of a pygmy anteater are made to tear open the tough nests of termites, on which it feeds. Those claws sank deeply into Walsh's wrist. Blood spurted from the gashes on his arm and he let out a cry. As the animal lifted its paws again, Walsh quickly stuffed it into a cage that was lying in the bottom of the boat. He had just learned a painful lesson that he would not forget.

This was the first of 161 pygmy anteaters that John Walsh was to capture during one of the most amazing rescue operations in history. The anteater, like thousands of other animals in the flooded South American jungle, was facing almost certain death.

But who is John Walsh? And why was he chosen to lead a daring rescue operation in a jungle that was as strange to him as it would have been to any other young man who had never been out of North America?

Wherever John Walsh is found, there is likely to be an animal nearby. This has been the case since he was a small boy growing up in Newton, Massachusetts. Newton is close to Boston, and one would not expect to find much woodland there today. But not so many years ago, when John Walsh was a boy, there were many wild areas near his home. Along the Charles River he found miles of swamps, woods, and sandpits to explore. And in those places he came across animals that fascinated him. Young John caught tadpoles, frogs, turtles. Once he found a nest of baby squirrels that had been abandoned by their mother. He took the squirrels home and kept them alive by feeding them night and day. When they were strong enough and old enough to care for themselves, he turned them loose in the woods.

Of all the wild creatures he found along the river, none interested John as much as snakes. He would catch various types of snakes and take them home with him. He learned to care for them properly, so that they were healthy and content in the cages he built for them. Even rattlesnakes!

"I still go looking for rattlesnakes," Walsh says. "There aren't many areas left in Massachusetts where you can find rattlesnakes today. But I know about a place where they live in dens in the hillside. I always go there on the first warm day of spring. The sun warms the rocks and the rattlesnakes come out of their dens. I don't catch them anymore. There aren't many of them left, so I just take color pictures of them."

It takes a special kind of person to feel that there is room in the world even for rattlesnakes. John Walsh was that kind of a boy. He never wanted to do anything else in life except work with animals. When he attended Boston University, he studied *biology*—the science that deals with living things.

"At first I thought the best kind of job would be to work as a forest ranger," Walsh says. "Most of the fellows I took biology with in school were going on to work in laboratories on research projects. But I didn't want to work in a lab. I wanted to get out in the woods and work with living animals."

Walsh had an idea that the life of a forest ranger was a glamorous one. But when he looked into the matter, he found that this was not always the case. Rangers in national forests or in national parks spend much of their time trying to keep people, rather than animals, out of trouble. And many of these rangers are cooped up in offices, filling out forms or writing reports.

"Their work is important," Walsh says, "but I wanted to be working directly with animals themselves. I know that civilization has caused animals a lot of problems that they can't deal with. I went around and asked many people for advice. Finally someone told me that I might be happiest working in a private wildlife sanctuary. Many people who are interested in animals give money to these wildlife sanctuaries. Often these sanctuaries have more money to devote to helping the animals than parks run by the state or the federal government."

Walsh found a successful wildlife sanctuary on Bear Island in New Hampshire's Lake

An MSPCA officer wears a gun and uniform like those of a state trooper.

Winnipesaukee. He learned that it was operated by the Massachusetts Society for the Prevention of Cruelty to Animals. This organization is often called the SPCA for short.

"I'd heard about the SPCA, of course," Walsh says. "I guess I had the same sort of notion about it that a lot of other people have—you know, that it's a sort of 'doggy-woggy, pussy-wussy' outfit."

But Walsh decided to pay a visit to the SPCA's office in Boston. That visit changed his life.

"When I got to the SPCA," Walsh remembers, "I saw some cars that looked like state police cars parked out in front. And when I walked inside I saw some fellows wearing uniforms that looked just like a state trooper's uniform. They even carried guns in holsters. The only thing different was their insignia, which read 'SPCA' instead of 'State Police.'"

103

Walsh learned that these men were enforcement officers for the SPCA. They had received special training from the state police. It was their duty to arrest and take to court people whom they found treating animals in a cruel manner. When they were working on a case, they were permitted to eat their meals with state troopers at any barracks in Massachusetts.

As Walsh soon learned, it is not easy to become an SPCA officer. The SPCA would not hire a person until he had gained a background in *veterinary medicine*—the science of treating sick and injured animals.

"You have to know a lot about animal diseases if you're going to be in a position to arrest people for cruelty," Walsh says. "Suppose you get a call from a woman who says her neighbor is starving his dog. Well, suppose that dog is really loaded with worms, or has some other disease that keeps it from putting on weight. Maybe its owner feeds it all right, but doesn't realize it's sick. So you've got to be able to examine the dog and find out just what is the matter with it before you go around arresting people."

Walsh had come to the right place. He decided to take the necessary training and become an enforcement officer. He began his training at the SPCA's Angell Memorial Hospital, the largest animal hospital in the world. It stands three stories high and covers almost a block in the city of Boston. A staff of about twenty-five veterinarians is always ready to treat animals in trouble. They are among the best in the business at their spe-

MSPCA officer John Walsh feeds a recuperating bird.

cialties. For instance, one is famous as an animal heart specialist. Another is an eye specialist. And there are veterinarians who treat only one kind of animal—a cat specialist, a bird specialist, even a monkey specialist! What Walsh learned at the hospital was to help make his rescue operation a great success when he went to the jungle several years later.

He began working in the hospital's wards, which are rooms in which the animals are treated and kept. He learned that there are separate wards in which dogs are treated for different diseases. There is a special ward for dogs that are being treated for contagious viruses, and another for dogs that are being treated for skin diseases. There are wards for horses and cows, wards for birds, and wards for snakes.

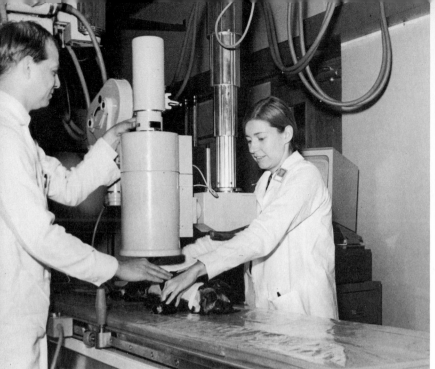

Technicians x-ray a Boston terrier at Angell Memorial Hospital.

It was Walsh's job to take care of the animals in the wards, just as a nurse might take care of human patients. He exercised the animals, took their temperatures, and made sure that they swallowed their pills. If the animals did not want to eat, he had to put the food in their mouths.

And all the time he kept his eyes open. He learned to identify types of diseases and what medicines to use in treating them. After a while he began to recognize the changes that take place in an animal as it grows worse or better.

After Walsh had worked in all the wards, he was sent to work in the clinic. This is the room to which people bring their animals if they are sick or hurt. If a man's dog has been hit by an automobile, or has a sore on its face, he can bring it to the clinic at Angell

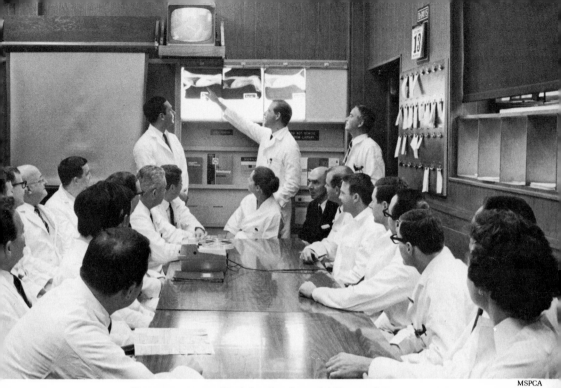

X rays are studied in the hospital's conference room.

Memorial Hospital. There, six veterinarians are on duty twenty-four hours a day.

Walsh was told to assist one of the doctors. It was his job to hold the animal on a table while the doctor examined it. If the doctor decided that there was nothing seriously wrong with the animal and it simply needed some medicine, Walsh would get the medicine and give it to the animal's owner.

But sometimes the doctor decided that the animal must remain in the hospital. He would tell his assistant what the trouble was, and then Walsh would take the animal to the X-ray room or to the proper ward. Walsh soon learned to tell if an animal had suffered a broken bone, and he would know exactly where the break had occurred and what kind of splint was needed.

107

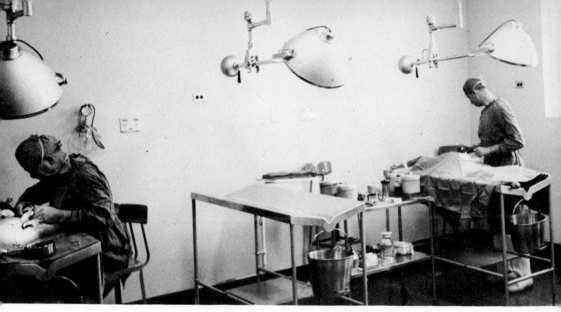

Major operations are performed by veterinarians in "sterile surgery."

Walsh also worked in the hospital pharmacy, where medicines are kept. It was his job to give these medicines to people whose pets were sick. By this time he had learned what questions to ask the people who came to the pharmacy. If he knew how an animal was behaving, and what its temperature was, he could tell a person what sort of medicine his pet needed. If the same person returned after several days or several weeks, he asked more questions. Had the medicine helped the animal? If it had not helped, Walsh might suggest another medicine.

As part of his training, Walsh spent three months working in "unsterile surgery." This is the room where simple operations are performed. Minor wounds are cleaned and dressed. Stitches are put in larger wounds. Animals are prepared for major operations. And, after they have been operated on, they are cared for there until they are out of danger.

At first, Walsh helped the veterinarians

with these tasks. Later, when his hands became as expert as those of the "vets," he performed many of these tasks himself. He put splints on broken bones, bandaged wounds, and examined his patients for all sorts of injuries and ills.

Next, Walsh was sent to work in "sterile surgery." Here major operations are performed under conditions in which few germs can live. All instruments are carefully sterilized. The veterinarian and his assistants wear caps and gowns and rubber gloves.

Walsh was one of these assistants. He remained in the operating room all day long. He scrubbed, ran errands for the vet, and handed him instruments during surgery.

Walsh watched fascinating operations. One of the veterinarians he most liked to watch at work was a woman who did heart surgery. She once performed open-heart surgery on a dog and a cat at the same time. And another time he saw her remove large worms that had infested the heart of a dog.

He watched in amazement as another vet removed a tumor from the wing of a parrakeet. This was a very delicate operation, for a small bird will die if it loses only a few drops of blood.

And Walsh watched in admiration as a veterinarian put metal pins in the wing of a hawk. The bird's wing had been shattered by a hunter's bullet. After the operation the hawk was put in a cage until the bones of the wing had mended.

"I was there when the bird was released," Walsh says. "We tossed him into the air and

A professional tree climber and John Walsh soothe a rescued cat.

he flapped his wings and flew off into the woods. There's a great feeling of satisfaction when you've worked with an animal for a long time and finally you watch it heal and go back to living its normal life." After his training in the operating room, John Walsh was put on his own. He was sent to "Rescue 8"—the SPCA department that rescues animals in trouble.

Rescue 8 has a fleet of trucks designed to hold dogs, cats, and other animals. Handling animals, even pets, can be hazardous if they are sick or in trouble. In their work, the men of Rescue 8 use different kinds of equipment to keep from being clawed or bitten. One item is the Ketch-All Pole. This is an aluminum pole five feet long. Some of the poles have extensions, making them fifteen feet long, if needed. A cable is strung through the pole, with a rubber-covered noose at its end.

110

John Walsh returns a mother duck to her family.

If an animal looks dangerous, or does not want to be picked up, the noose can be slipped over its head and tightened. The animal can neither run away nor attack the man at the other end of the pole and can then be guided into a cage.

Mink handlers' gloves are also part of Rescue 8's standard equipment. These are large mittens made of several layers of leather. They were developed for handling mink, which can bite through an ordinary glove. These gloves protect a man's arm all the way up to the elbow.

Tranquilizer guns are also particularly handy for SPCA workers. These unusual guns fire darts instead of bullets. In the dart is a drug that puts an animal to sleep. When the dart enters the body of an animal it does not cause a painful wound, but produces only a pinprick.

Every day people call the SPCA to report animals in trouble or that have become nuisances:

> A cat is up a telephone pole and can't get down.
>
> A squirrel is running between the walls of somebody's house.
>
> A skunk has knocked over a garbage pail and is making a mess.
>
> A mad dog is running through the streets.

"We always get lots of calls about raccoons," Walsh says. "Especially in early spring, before the leaves are on the trees—people are always looking up and seeing a raccoon on a branch.

" 'There's a raccoon up my tree,' somebody will tell us on the phone. 'What shall I do?'

"We tell them that this is only natural. Raccoons move around at night. When daylight comes they crawl up into a tree and go to sleep.

"But it's different when a raccoon gets into somebody's attic. The reason a raccoon goes there is to build a nest. Then we have to go and get it out—and that's not always so easy. A raccoon isn't very cooperative. It doesn't want to go with you. Even with heavy gloves on we're always getting bitten."

At last John Walsh was ready to be trained in law enforcement. Massachusetts has a number of laws that protect animals from cruel treatment. Walsh found that this was the most complicated part of his job, for in law enforcement he had to deal with people as well as with animals.

After rescuing a gamecock from an illegal cockfight, Walsh and a fellow officer remove the artificial spurs from its legs.

"You learn this side of the job by traveling with an enforcement officer for several months," Walsh says. "Then you go to the police academy for special training in learning how to arrest people. You also learn how to protect yourself in case the fellow you are trying to arrest decides to attack you. Finally you take a college course to learn about law and how to take lawbreakers to court."

In 1961 Walsh completed his training and joined the Law Enforcement Department of the Massachusetts SPCA. He had wanted to help animals, but until he joined the SPCA he had not realized how much animals really needed help.

Every day his chief sent him on a new adventure. Most investigations of cruelty to animals are prompted by complaints of private citizens. In winter Walsh would investigate many cases of animals that suffered from the cold. Perhaps a farmer had not given his cows and horses shelter during a blizzard. Perhaps a woman had left her dog outdoors all night in freezing weather.

Walsh, who became used to investigating cases of cruelty to animals, was shocked by many of the things he saw. He arrested a man who poisoned some dogs simply because they had trampled his flower garden. He once caught some boys who had poured lighter fluid on a cat and then set fire to it.

Walsh investigated every complaint made to his office. If he found that the complaint was true, he took the guilty person to court. In Massachusetts, a person found guilty of being cruel to animals may be fined by the judge. If his act is serious enough, he may be sent to prison.

As an SPCA officer, Walsh often visited horse shows, dog shows, county fairs, circuses, and rodeos.

"There's a lot of animal suffering connected with a rodeo," he says. "Sometimes when a cowboy bulldogs a steer, he sticks his fingers in the animal's eyes to make it fall down fast. And just before they send out the bucking bronco they sometimes stick nails— or some kind of hot chemical—in the strap that goes around its belly. This irritates the horse and makes it buck higher."

Walsh found he must always be prepared for trouble. Several times, when a man has been caught torturing an animal, he has threatened Walsh.

"But you carry a pistol with you," Walsh says, "and if necessary you can bend it between somebody's ears and then he listens to you."

At times like that, his job is not very pleasant. But he has had rewards at other times. Among the places he inspects for cruelty are pet shops. Although owners of pet shops may not mean to be cruel, Walsh explains, they often fail to care for their animals out of sheer ignorance. Sometimes, on weekends, owners go away and leave animals sitting in cages in the windows. If the sun grows very warm, they may die.

But it was in a pet shop that John Walsh met a delightful creature named Susie. She was a sun bear from Malaysia.

"As soon as I walked into this pet shop I didn't like the looks of it," Walsh says. "The cages were dirty and the animals didn't look very healthy. Then I went into the back room and saw a sun bear. She was only a cub, but she was all hunched up in a cage that was much too small for her. And she was half-starved—all skin and bones."

Walsh took the sun bear to Angell Memorial Hospital, where the veterinarians fed it vitamins and good food. Soon the bear was healthy, but no one knew what to do with it. If Susie stayed too long at the hospital she might catch a disease from another animal. The Boston zoo already owned a sun bear and had no room for another. What could the SPCA do with a growing sun bear that already stood three feet tall?

John Walsh said he would keep her in his apartment until a new home could be found for her.

"She was housebroken, no problem at all," he says. "My apartment was right at the end of a dead-end street. Most of the people who lived around me were old folks, and they didn't know who was living with me."

Walsh found her to be a wonderful roommate. Early in the morning, before he went to work, he put Susie in his car and drove her out to the woods, where they took long walks together. In the evenings Walsh and Susie often wrestled on the living room floor.

"She wouldn't hurt anybody," he says. "Oh, she'd scratch me sometimes. But she was just a big slob."

The happy home was broken up one day when Walsh let her roam in the backyard. An old lady who lived nearby came out to empty her garbage. Susie loved garbage. She ran over to the woman and, with one quick swipe of her paw, plucked the garbage from her hand.

"It took me quite a while to calm that old lady down," Walsh says.

Soon after that, he found a home for Susie on a farm in New Hampshire.

But, as a rule, John Walsh does not think it is right to keep wild animals as pets.

"You can't really *possess* a wild animal," he says. "Some people, for instance, like to capture baby raccoons and raise them in the house. They're cute when they're tiny. But in a year they grow up, and soon they weigh about fifty pounds. You can't tell what they'll do. They'll bite you and they'll bite hard. They don't mean to hurt you—it's just their nature because they don't want to be picked up. It's the only way they have of telling you. Other wild animals are the same way."

Although he had many experiences with animals that either lived or belonged in the wild, John Walsh was concerned mostly with domestic animals. In cases of cruel treatment he usually found that it was more rewarding to win people over by persuasion rather than force. He often attended local fairs, where a great attraction was the horse-pulling contest. The owners of horses would compete to see whether or not one man's horse could pull a heavier load than a neighbor's. Sometimes an owner would hide a nail in his hand and push on the horse's rump. The nail would stick into the horse and it would move ahead, pulling a greater weight than it was built to move.

"The first prize in these contests was usually fifty dollars," Walsh says. "So I would go around to the local merchants and get them to put up a prize for the most *humane* owner, and it got so that this prize was worth more than fifty dollars. So the owners stopped torturing their horses and went out to win the humane prize. I think everybody was happier—especially the horses!"

Meanwhile, certain events were taking place in South America that would change John Walsh's life once more. To provide water for electric power, a great dam had been built by an aluminum company on a river in Surinam. Formerly called Dutch Guiana, this small country is on the northern coast of South America. In February, 1964,

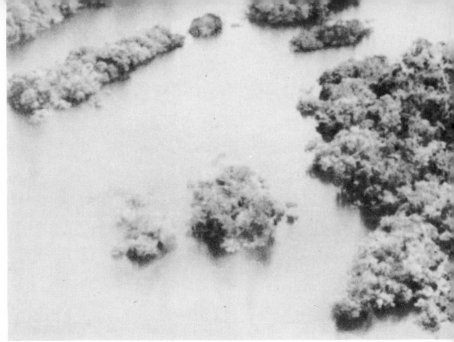

the dam was closed. The water in the Surinam River began to form a huge lake that spread rapidly and flooded 870 square miles of jungle. Birds, of course, were able to fly out of the area. But many animals—deer, sloths, monkeys, snakes, anteaters, and jaguars—were in danger of being drowned. Those that were not drowned would die of starvation when their food was destroyed by the rising water.

Many people in Surinam knew that something had to be done quickly. They wrote a letter to the International Society for the Protection of Animals requesting help. This organization, called ISPA for short, has offices in Boston and in London, England. The people in Surinam concluded their letter with an eloquent plea: "Time is short and the water rises." Moved by the letter, the ISPA officials in Boston began to look for a man to conduct a large-scale rescue effort.

118

The flooded Surinam area.

In a way, Santa Claus helped the ISPA find the man to rescue the animals. Every winter in Massachusetts, there were a number of Christmas displays in which a Santa Claus rode in a sleigh pulled by several reindeer. Sometimes one of the animals would escape from the display. In that case, the owner of the reindeer always called the SPCA, and John Walsh was sent to look for the animal. Walsh carried a tranquilizer gun on these hunts. When he found the reindeer, he "shot" it and put it to sleep. Then the animal was put in a truck and returned to its owner.

The officers of the International Society for the Protection of Animals had formed a plan for the rescue effort in Surinam. They wanted someone to go into the jungle and capture as many animals as possible. Some could be caught by hand or in nets, and others would have to be "shot" with a tran-

119

ISPA

A tranquilizer gun fires a dart that puts an animal to sleep.

quilizer gun. All the animals that were captured could be taken out of the flooded region and set free again.

It was a daring plan. No one had ever tried anything like this in a great area of jungle, and no one knew if it would work. But the ISPA had heard of John Walsh and his skill with a tranquilizer gun.

Walsh's chief at the SPCA agreed to lend him to the International Society for the project. When the society asked him if he was interested in Surinam, he had to admit that he didn't even know what they were talking about. Was Surinam a special kind of boat? Was it a special kind of toad? But it wasn't long before his ignorance was cleared up and he found himself in this beautiful little country, mixed up in the greatest adventure of his life.

120

men swam after this deer when canoes could not get through the brush.

There were some people who said that the job could not be done in the thick jungle. Other people said that all the animals had already moved out of the region and there would be nothing to catch. But when Walsh took a trip through the jungle, he believed that many animals were still there.

After he had toured the flooded region, Walsh made his own plans. He hired Bush Negroes to help him. At first they could not understand what he was trying to do. The Bush Negroes had always thought of animals simply as food. In fact, their name for animals was the same as their name for food—*gwamba*. But after the rescue effort had gotten under way, they became so involved that they often risked their lives to help Walsh. They had a special name for the project—Operation Gwamba.

Walsh and his men put bound animals into dugout canoes.

Walsh was not able to buy the boats he needed, so he had dugout boats constructed by the Bush Negroes. He also had to obtain twenty outboard motors for them, and enough fuel to keep them running for nine hours a day.

Walsh brought with him from Boston much of the equipment he had used as an officer for the SPCA. He brought his tranquilizer guns, of course. He also brought the special poles and nets for catching the animals, and the thick gloves for handling them without being bitten.

Operation Gwamba was tiring work. Walsh and his men were in their boats many hours a day, searching the jungle for animals.

Wearing heavy gloves, John Walsh holds a snowy owl.

They constantly drew maps of the area that would show them where the water was rising the highest. Then they would go to that place. Some of the men went through the jungle in teams, using dogs to drive the animals before them. Finally the animals—deer, anteaters, tapirs, and others—would be driven into the water.

Whenever Walsh saw an animal swimming, he headed his boat in its direction. It was a difficult job to grab a large, frightened creature in the water, tie it up, and haul it into the boat. Often Walsh and his men plunged into the water themselves. They were often kicked in the stomach by flailing hoofs and scratched by flashing claws.

Piranhas were a constant danger in this region. These small fish swim in great swarms and attack any living thing they find in the water. They are able to tear all the flesh off the body of a man or a horse in minutes. Once, as Walsh's boat sped through the flooded jungle, one of his helpers trailed his hand idly in the water. Suddenly the man let out a scream. He pulled his hand from the water and saw that a piranha had bitten off the end of his finger!

In the evenings, Walsh and his men made camp and ate their dinner. It was not a very appetizing meal—usually rice and pig tails. Walsh found pig tails were handy because they could be kept for several weeks in the jungle without spoiling. He simply chopped them up with a machete—a large, heavy knife used in South America. Then he put the chunk of tail into his mouth, sucked the meat off it, and spit out the bone.

After dinner Walsh would treat the sick and injured animals he had captured. Then he would look over the maps. In places where the water was highest, he knew that it had probably killed the trees and bushes. He would have to work fast, for there was nothing left in those places for the animals to eat. The only advantage was that he would be able to see the animals in the trees because most of the leaves had fallen.

By this time, Walsh and his men were capturing between twenty and fifty animals a day. Sometimes the animals he found were nearly dead from starvation. He kept a number of cans of fruit cocktail in the boat

Christine Snook

Every evening John Walsh treated the sick animals.

because he had learned that starving animals were able to swallow it easily. Some animals were too weak to eat, however, so Walsh developed a clever way of feeding them. He took the tube that carried gas from the tank to the outboard motor, washed it out, and thrust it down the animals' throats. Then he poured fruit cocktail into the tube. Through these force-feedings, starving animals were soon strong enough to eat on their own.

125

At first even the Bush Negroes who worked with him did not understand why he wanted to save the animals. But soon they were working just as hard as he was to pick some tired and struggling creature from the rising water. However, one man who worked for the aluminum company used to tease Walsh about the rescue operation.

"What are you wearing yourself out for just to save some animals?" he would ask Walsh.

One day Walsh gave him a ride in his boat. As they were cruising through the jungle, they spied a three-fingered sloth. It was clinging to a branch just above the water. Walsh picked up the helpless creature, then put it back on the branch. Without looking

Walsh holds an ocelot by the skin of its neck to avoid being clawed.

ISPA

back, he turned and headed the boat in another direction.

"Hey, what are you doing?" the man cried. "Aren't you going to save that animal?"

Walsh shook his head. "Why bother?"

"But you can't leave it there to die!" the man shouted. "Turn around!"

Walsh, grinning, went back and rescued the sloth. Someone else had been made to understand.

When Operation Gwamba was concluded, one reporter called it "a tremendous success—the most efficient wildlife rescue operation ever to take place anywhere in the world."

"At first we figured we'd be able to rescue about three thousand animals before the

"Operation Gwamba" rescued a total of 2,104 three-toed sloths.

Dr. G. van der lingen

water reached its full height," Walsh says. "As it was, we saved more than nine thousand."

After leading Operation Gwamba, John Walsh remained with ISPA. This organization was formed in 1959 to save animals, not just in the United States, but all over the world. Walsh now directs ISPA's field rescue operations in North and South America. He travels many thousands of miles on missions like the following:

The annual seal hunt in the Pribilof Islands of the northern Pacific Ocean. Here fifty thousand fur seals are killed every year for their skins. Walsh tries to see that they do not suffer needlessly.

Conferences of the International Whaling Commission. Whaling ships still search the seas for whales—the world's largest mammals. Walsh hopes that laws and treaties to protect them can be passed before all the whales are killed.

Slaughterhouses in South America. Many animals such as hogs and steers are taken to slaughterhouses and butchered with great cruelty. Walsh works for more humane conditions in this industry.

John Walsh believes that the best hope for rescuing animals from cruel treatment and, in many cases, extinction lies with young people. He takes part in educational programs that teach children a reverence for all living things.

"Programs that teach the care of the cat and the dog are fine in the United States and Canada," Walsh says. "But conditions are

Including this small variety, a total of 1,061 armadillos were rescued.

different in other countries. In some sections of South America we teach children how to load donkeys with firewood or how to hitch them to wagons without hurting them."

Walsh and other ISPA officers carry on this type of work through lectures, books, and films. He hopes that many young people will want to make a career of working with animals.

"This is an exciting and a rewarding field," John Walsh says. "I think it's the best job in the world."

Authors' Note

The next time the reader sees a flock of geese flying high overhead, or sees a deer bound across the road in front of a car, we hope he will think of the people in this book. For the work of Guy Bradley, Margaret Owings, Herbert Johnson, and John Walsh clearly show what is needed if we are to preserve the wild things that are left to us.

Here is a list of books and articles that we found helpful as we wrote this book:

CHAPTER 1—"The Cruise of the Bonton," by Charles W. Pierce. (Printed in *Tequesta*, the Journal of the Historical Association of Southern Florida, No. XXLL, 1962.)
The Roseate Spoonbill, by Robert Porter Allen. (Published by the National Audubon Society, 1942.)

CHAPTER 2—*Otters*, by C. J. Harris. (Published by Weidenfeld and Nicolson, London, 1968.)

CHAPTER 3—*The Natural History of New York City*, by John Kieran. (Published by Houghton Mifflin Company, 1959.)

CHAPTER 4—*Time Is Short and the Water Rises*, by John Walsh and Robert Gannon. (Published by E. P. Dutton, 1967.)

INDEX

Page numbers in italics refer to pictures.

About the Authors

Frank Graham, Jr., is a field editor of *Audubon* magazine and a prominent writer of conservation books, including *Since Silent Spring*. He has also written a number of books for young people, including *Austria* and *Margaret Chase Smith, Woman of Courage*. His wife, Ada, is a teacher who is also the author (with her husband) of a book for young people about the food industry entitled *The Great American Shopping Cart*. The Grahams live in Milbridge, Maine.